A STEP-BY-STEP GUIDE TO RAISING
GUINEA FOWL
ON A SMALL SCALE

GARDENING
WITH
GUINEAS

JEANNETTE S. FERGUSON

D0596851

*...The world would be a very silent place,
if no birds sang except those who sang best. ***

Gardening With Guineas
COPYRIGHT © 1999 by Jeannette S. Ferguson
All rights reserved.

FFE MEDIA • P.O. Box 804 • Waynesville, OH • 45068-0804

Library of Congress Control Number: 99-94530
ISBN: 0-7392-0250-2
Sixteenth Printing 2006

****

Some of the illustrations in this book are true to life and are included with the permission of the persons involved. All others are composites of real situations and any resemblance to people living or dead is coincidental.

Information in this book should be considered only a guide. Individual situations will vary. Many over-the-counter medications are not approved for use on Guinea Fowl. The guinea fowl breeder accepts full responsibility for such use and will hold harmless the writer, manufacturers and those that sell any such medications. Always follow the directions on the label.
****

Cover Photograph by Carien Quiroga
* Adapted from *Bernard Meltzer's Guidance for Living* by Bernard Meltzer

Ferguson, Jeannette S.
    Gardening with guineas: a step-by-step guide to raising guinea fowl on a small scale / Jeannette S. Ferguson
1.Guinea Fowl   2.Gardening   3.Poultry   I.Title

Printed in the USA by

MORRIS PUBLISHING
3212 East Highway 30 • Kearney, NE 68847 • 1-800-650-7888

Contents

Contents

To my precious children Zachary and Olivia,
Who gave up quality time so that I could work on this book.

And to my husband Jim,
Who took this country girl out of the city.

Acknowledgments

Writing this book would not have been possible without the support I received from many, many online friends. By way of my website on the World Wide Web, I was able to create an interactive Guinea Fowl Message Board, where regular visitors as well as new ones gave me the confidence I needed to to complete this project. I wish to thank each and every one of you who have shared questions and comments. I would also like to express my deep appreciation to the following people in my life, who have given me the extra push I needed to write this book.

To my good friend and mentor, Karen E. VanMackelberg, whose patience and excellent computer skills showed me the way more times than I care to admit.

To my editor Ellen R. Patton, for her continuous words of support and for being available when I needed her.

To my husband Jim, who built the henhouse, and modifies it as I make changes, who supports my hobbies and cares for the guineas when I need help.

To my parents, Ray and Esther McClain, who raised me to believe I can do anything I want, as long as the desire is there and I don't just sit back and wait for things to happen.

And a very special thanks to author Jayne Schooler, who was the main person responsible for guiding me in the right direction and giving me the kick I needed to "follow my dream" by turning my thoughts of writing this book into a reality.

Introduction

As an avid gardener and member of the local Garden Club, my desire was to be able to participate in the flower show at our county fair, but it just couldn't happen. My beautiful gardens were bug infested by fair time in mid July. Japanese Beetles took over, engulfing my roses, as many as twenty inside a single rose bud! Grasshoppers chewed holes in what seemed to be every leaf not damaged by some other sort of insect. It was heartbreaking.

You see, I live in the country on a small 14-acre farm with fields on either side. To hire a lawn care company or to use chemicals myself to control bugs and weeds was neither a desire nor an option.

Ticks were thick. A walk across the yard to gather berries, work in the vegetable garden or simply to pick a few flowers for the table would nearly guarantee my discovery of a tick hiding behind an ear or in the hair on my head during my evening shower and shampoo. The thought of someone in my family getting Lyme Disease from a tick bite was horrifying to me. Something had to be done.

During a garden club meeting at a member's home, my attention wandered from the speaker to outside the window where plump, speckled birds were dashing across the yard like little roadrunners. Their little legs were moving at what seemed to be a hundred miles an hour, yet their bodies were so very still! The antics of these beautiful birds were most humorous to watch.

I couldn't wait until that meeting was over to get an even better look and to question the homeowner about these hilarious creatures.

After discovering that guineas not only eat ticks, but also mosquitoes, Japanese Beetles, and weed seeds, I left that meeting with a big smile on my face and six guinea eggs in my pocket. A trip to the library the next morning resulted in a failure to find virtually anything about raising guineas. As a result of my own knowledge and experience, I felt compelled to write this step by step guide for others who desire to garden with these wonderful birds and to PROMOTE THE GUINEA.

Chapter

1

The Basics

FIRST THINGS FIRST

Before jumping in feet first, it is a good idea to know just what is in store for you when raising any animal, and to know some of the basic characteristics of the species. This chapter will fill you in on some of the history, terminology, and technical information you should know ahead of time if you plan to raise and breed guinea fowl.

REASONS FOR RAISING GUINEA FOWL

Guinea fowl are truly beautiful birds. Most, including the white, have at least a few spots, appearing more like tiny squares than dots. These unusual feathers, especially those of the pearl guinea fowl, are often used in hats and for crafts such as Dream Catchers and decorative gourds. I have also used them in the artistic design section of the local flower show in arrangements.

The entertainment guineas provide is reason enough to own a few. They are quite humorous to watch as they dart across the yard like little roadrunners. It is comical to watch the common practice of two males in chase during the mating season. Holding their bodies level with wings up and back, only their legs appear to be moving at what seems to be an abnormally quick rate. They will continue the chase until one wears down, leaving the other to become the soul mate for a particular guinea hen.

Seniors, children, and even any salesmen frequenting the farm always take notice of the guinea fowl running around on the property, and often comment in favor of the enjoyment they have received from just watching the guineas in action. Bird watching is quite an interesting hobby in itself, and surely the guinea fowl is one of the most humorous to observe. When all is calm, it is very relaxing just to sit and watch them parading across the lawn. My feathered friends have been good for my heart and soul and a link back to the basics of farm living.

Guineas are often referred to as the farmer's watchdog. When on free range, they come to know just who does and does not belong on your property. The adult guinea is normally quiet unless disturbed, but watch out! At the first sign of a hawk, raccoon, coyote, fox, skunk opossum, stray dog, fox or poacher, etc. you will surely be warned! The shrill call of the guinea is a warning to the other animals on the farm, and is often enough to frighten away the intruder. If you hear a commotion, you can be sure something is out there.

Here on the farm, when we hear the guineas making a commotion, we always look out to see what is happening. Once it was a coyote running right past my son!!!!! I was working in my greenhouse at the time. My son was on the swing set just outside. I looked up in time to see the coyote run down the fence row just outside the greenhouse!

More common is the overhead hawk. The warning call of the guineas notifies the chickens who then dash inside the hen house immediately! The guineas duck under pine trees, the hawk flies off, and soon the excitement is over.

The barn cats and family dog will soon learn not to bother the guineas. On my farm, GUINEAS RULE! After a time, they get used to each other and get along fine. At first, the sound of the guineas will often be enough to intimidate the dogs and cats to turn tail and run. However, if you have a dog trained to hunt and kill birds, this would not be the case. Once a dog has a taste of blood for killing birds, it will not stop. Guineas will range right through the goat yard and cow pasture with no problems whatsoever.

Guineas detest snakes, and will kill any they find! Once snakes were commonly seen slithering through my flowerbeds or hanging on a plant. Now the only snakes I have seen have been dead ones! The free-ranging guineas kill the snakes then leave them laying for me to find.

Guinea Fowl can be a source of limited income for the small farmer. The money generated from the sale of extra keets and fertile eggs covers the cost of additional feed for chickens as well as supplies needed for either. This is not to mention the money saved by not purchasing weed or insect sprays.

Guinea eggs can be eaten just as chicken eggs and should be collected daily for food consumption. During the laying season, one can expect an egg a day from a good hen. Although their brown eggs are not as large as hen eggs, what they lack in size, they make up for in quality. Guinea eggs whites beat up light and fluffy and are excellent in cake baking.

Guinea meat is tender, dark, and fine game-type flavored having a high meat-to-bone ratio. The meat of the white guinea is said to be lighter. Guinea fowl meat is leaner and drier than chicken meat. Finer gourmet restaurants and hotels who specialize in bird meat may list guinea on the menu. Those who serve game bird will, at times, substitute guinea meat when they run short supply of pheasant. Guinea fowl can be sized and prepared to eat or market at 14 to 16 weeks.

A specialty restaurant in Indiana contacted me with regards to supplying them with guinea fowl meat. However, my small farm raises a homestead flock, and I am not set up to raise enormous amounts of guineas to supply a restaurant at this time. Although with 14 acres we do have room to expand and build a guinea fowl hatchery, neither my family nor I want to jump into a new career at this point in our lives, nor do we have the desire to become a supplier of guinea fowl for restaurants. Suppliers are few, and can be in great demand in the right area.

Raising guinea fowl can be an individual hobby, a 4-H project to teach children responsibility, or just for the pride of ownership, companionship, or for a specific purpose such as to aid in organic gardening.

Beneficial to the lawn itself is the guano. Unlike a pile of dog feces, you won't have to worry about stepping in a big pile of guinea guano. In fact, even when keeping an eye out, it is very seldom noticed, if at all. Guinea guano is high in nitrates making it an excellent free fertilizer. The droppings are non-offensive, and messy only if the bird is ill. Guinea guano is basically dry, and washes away easily in the rain. Part of my drive is in blacktop, and it is extremely rare that I would ever find a pile on it or in my flowerbeds. (I wish I could say the same for dog or cat dung!) Besides, who can complain about free fertilizer?

The guinea fowl is the most active gardener on the farm. Continuously on the move, they pick up bugs and weed seeds with nearly every step they take. They will walk right through flowerbeds picking bugs off the plants as they go along, without harming a single tender leaf! They love moths, slugs, aphids, and grasshoppers too! Unlike chickens, guineas do not scratch, therefore do not harm delicate plants or flowers in gardens. Some of my plants and seedlings are fairly tender.

I start all of the flowers and vegetables on the farm from seed in my hobby greenhouse. With intentions of entering flower shows, believe me when I tell you I am very protective of my gardens! I would not think to have guinea fowl on my property if they did any damage to the gardens! They do not harm the gardens or flowers, but help them!

Guineas are a plus to fruit growers, grain farmers, and market gardeners. They will protect cherry trees and strawberry patches from raiding robins and other birds. Guineas are not destroyers, but one of the most active enemies to be found of insects, bugs, and weed seeds that are a nuisance to every gardener or farmer.

Gardening With Guineas is beneficial, enjoyable, and relaxing. My gardening companions are quite helpful and fun to garden with. They know me well, so I am not a distraction to them as they make their way through the gardens with me. It is nothing for me to be weeding and have one of them come up next to me and pick a potato bug off a plant or an insect off a flower.

I have coaxed guineas into my rose garden intentionally to help with my Japanese Beetle and slug problems. I must tell you, my guineas have done a great job on previously infested flowerbeds. I was able to enter our local sanctioned county flower show for the first time in years only <u>after</u> I began to raise guinea fowl. I commend my guineas for the 3 rosettes and 18 ribbons I won at my very first show. Even a rose of mine took Best of Show!

POPULAR COMMON BREEDS

The common farmer should know his guineas were originally from the Central African plains where they are still hunted as game birds. They have been traced back as far as the ancient Greeks and Romans where they were raised for table birds. Early settlers brought guineas to the United States.

Guinea fowl belong to the family Phasianidae of the order Galliformes. They are sometimes placed in their own family, Numididae. The species with a bushy tuft of feathers on the crown are classified in the genus *Guttera.* The helmeted guinea fowl is classified as *Numida meleagris,* its western African subspecies as *Numida meleagris galeata,* and the white-breasted guinea fowl as *Agelastes meleagrides.* The black guinea fowl is classified as *Agelastes niger* (sometimes *Phasidus niger*), and the vulturine guinea fowl as *Acryllium vulturinum.*[1]

The three most popular breeds in America are the Vulturine, Crested, and Helmeted Guinea Fowl.

---

[1]"Guinea Fowl," *Microsoft® Encarta® 96 Encyclopedia.* © 1993-1995 Microsoft Corporation. All rights reserved. © Funk & Wagnalls Corporation. All rights reserved.

The Vulturine Guinea Fowl (Acrylllium Vulturinum) is from the semi-arid regions of east Africa. The vulturine is not commonly raised on most farms, as it is more sensitive to cold and lacks the hardiness of the common guinea fowl. It has a helmetless head and does somewhat resemble the look of a vulture. Its body is about 24 inches long and tapering with longitudinally striped black and white plumes, cobalt blue skin and a bright aquiline colored head. It holds its entire body more at a diagonal angle than the common guinea fowl. It is an exotic bird, owned mainly by collectors and for show. In my search to locate vulturine guinea fowl, I found some with prices varying in the several hundreds of dollars a pair. Due to the expense of the bird, needless to say, I will not be purchasing them to free range on this farm. For me to own a pair of vulturine guinea fowl would require separate housing, and a huge enclosed run. This goes against my purpose in raising domesticated guinea fowl, which is *Gardening With Guineas*.

The Crested Guinea Fowl (Guttera Pucherani) has jet-black feathers which resembles a pouffy type haircut on its head. It has black collar-like hairs separating the white skin on its head from the rest of its body, which resembles the common guinea fowl. Kenya Crested Guineas can be purchased at a high price of a few hundred dollars per pair, a price tag usually lower than the vulturine guineas. A bird of this value is not practical for gardening.

The Helmeted Guinea Fowl (Numinidae Meleagris) is the most common breed of the species. It is quite inexpensive to purchase. The Portuguese brought these to Europe from Africa in the 15th Century. These have a bare head and neck, sleek body with a short tail, and smooth feathers. They are named for the bony casque on their head. Several subspecies, including the Central African guinea fowl have been long since domesticated. The domestic strains used to be the pearl gray, white, and lavender. However, now there are several other domestic varieties available. They come in many colors including royal purple, slate, coral blue, buff, buff dundotte, light blue, light lavender, opaline, porcelain, violet, chocolate, brown, powder blue, violet, bronze, pewter, sky blue, silver polished and white-breasted. White-breasted are often referred to as pied or tuxedo.

French guineas are listed by some hatcheries as being "The Roaster Guinea", ready for the table in 10 weeks. These are advertised as having pearl coloring, with hybrid vigor, large body and shorter neck. They are said to have more breast meat and to grow a bit larger. The French are priced a bit higher than the domestic guinea fowl.

CLASSIFICATION

A guinea fowl is not a chicken. The guinea fowl is more active, ranges further, and flies higher. A guinea is nearest to the wild of all of the so-called domestic fowl. Although they are also not game birds, they are most like them. Guinea can be hunted for sport such as a game bird, although there is no "open-season" on guinea fowl. Guineas can be domesticated like a chicken, and can be a table bird, such as peafowl.

The guinea fowl is a species of its own. Guineas are rough, vigorous, hardy, basically disease-free birds, having no diseases of their own. When members of 4-H clubs raise guineas or others show guineas in local fairs, they can be found housed with poultry.

In the United States Code of Federal Regulations, Title9, chapter 1, Subpart A Birds, Section 93.100 in the Animal and Plant Health Inspection Service, United States Department of Agriculture, lists poultry as follows:

Poultry. Chickens, doves, ducks, geese, grouse, guinea fowl, partridges, pea fowl, pheasants, pigeon, quail, swans, and turkeys (including eggs for hatching)

The guinea hen and the cock on the right are fully aware of the cats watching them. However, there is no need for alarm, as the barn cats on this farm have learned not to bother the guineas.

TERMINOLOGY

Many whom I have come in contact with tend to say, "Oh look at those guinea hens," grouping all guineas into one category. Those of us who raise guineas should know and use the proper terms for both the birds and their body parts. They are listed here for easy reference:

POULTRY: Domestic fowls raised for meat or eggs.

GUINEA FOWL: The proper name for the species.

BREED: Such as the Helmeted, Vulturine, Crested

VARIETIES: Differences in color patterns or markings

KEET: The offspring of a guinea hen & guinea cock ages birth through 12 weeks.

YOUNG GUINEA: Any guinea aged 12 - 52 weeks old.

PULLET: A female guinea under a year old

COCKEREL: A male guinea under a year old.

GUINEA COCK: An adult male guinea one year or older.

GUINEA HEN: Adult female guinea a year of age or older.

GROWTH:
12 weeks.........approximately 1.2 lbs.
16 weeks...........approximately 2.2 lbs.

Cock......................................3.0 - 3.5 lbs.
Cockerel................................3.0 lbs.
Hen.......................................3.5lbs.
Pullet....................................3.0 lbs.

Pictured are pearl, young guineas 6 months old.

BODY PARTS

HELMET: Commonly called the topknot, comb, or casque. It is a pale, waxy brown color (nearly black in young birds), hard, and curving toward the body

WATTLES: These are the fleshy coral red appendages that hang from either side of the head. Flat, stiff, free from wrinkles, the lower edge is curved from the beak. In the males, it is much larger and has a cupped appearance.

HEAD: Wedge-shaped and short, it tapers toward the beak. The head is covered with white skin with a line of very fine hair-like feathers down the back of the head sticking out and growing upward.

EYES: Very alert, large, round, dark brown

NECK: Rounded with down-like feathers

SHANKS: Legs, bright orange in keets, changing to mottled orange with brown, then black as older adults

TOES: Strong and straight

BEAK: Short, strong, and curved

WINGS: Large and carried horizontally

BACK: Broad curving from the neck descending gradually to the tail.

BODY: Long with a full, rounded breast

TAIL: Carried low to the ground, and is rather short

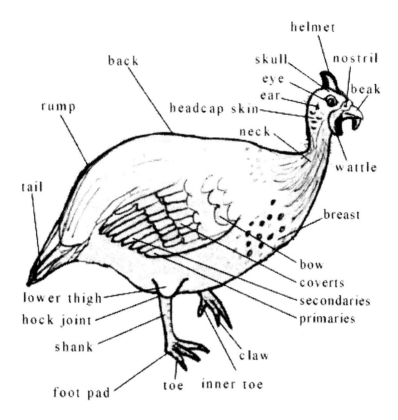

Now that you are familiar with reasons for raising guinea fowl and some of the background and technical information, you can jump right into the heart of the book about how to raise helmeted guinea fowl for pleasure and gardening.

2

Getting Started

BEFORE YOU BUY

If you now have the desire to raise some guineas, before you run out and grab the first one you can find, you need to prepare for them.

First, be certain you live in an area where raising guineas is permitted. Agricultural zoning is always acceptable, country living usually poses no problems. However, when in an area of closely confined housing, you need to be sure it is compatible with your zoning and any other restrictions for your area. Detailed Information in checking things out can be found in "Boundaries".

Guineas will range out and cross the boundaries of a small lot. It would be courteous to discuss your intentions with any close neighbors in advance if you want to avoid any unforeseen complaints from them. Give them a bit of history on the bird, and share with them the value of these meat eaters. Most neighbors should welcome these bug eaters whom they will have no responsibility for, yet reap the rewards from. It seems odd to me that anyone would live in an area properly zoned for raising agricultural animals, then turn around and complain should one cross onto their property. Unfortunately, this can happen. Most who live in the country realize that fencing does break down, animals do get loose, and "things happen". Living in the country, I have had neighbor's cows, dogs and cats, wild deer, coyote, fox, opossum, raccoons, rabbits, hawks, owls and Canadian geese, to name a few, in my yard. All are damaging intruders, quite unlike guinea fowl. However, they are silent intruders, whereas the guinea fowl can be noisy at times, especially when disturbed.

So far so good - no unforeseen problems? OK. The next step is to be certain you have the proper housing before you get your guineas.

THE ADULT HOME

Guineas need shelter from high winds, rain, cold, and sun as well as a place to roost that is safe from predators. Building a home for them or making room in a pre-existing barn or shed is the first step. As it happens, I also have a few chickens I raise for eggs and a rooster for his crow. (Personally, I just could not imagine living in the country and not awaking to hear the sound of a rooster.) My guineas roost in a henhouse with them.

THE HENHOUSE AND EQUIPMENT

My particular hen house happens to be a section in the back of a shed with an attached greenhouse on one side. The potting shed is the storage area for both my greenhouse supplies and chicken/guinea feed. I store the feed in standard 50-gallon tough plastic trash containers with tight fitting lids to keep out mice and other intruders. The plastic does not rust at the seams, as the metal containers eventually will. The entire shed has a wood floor, which is also safer for both my birds and the storage area.

An alternative is to have a one-room henhouse with no separate storage area. If the food must be stored inside the henhouse, choose containers that to not have handles of any sort. Guineas as well as chickens love to sit up high and will get on top of that container! When I first started raising chickens, one morning I walked into my henhouse to find a rooster hanging upside down by his leg which had slipped through the handle of a feed container inside the coop. What a sight that was, but he let me lift him out with no fighting! Luckily he was just fine.

The entrance to the henhouse is from inside the potting shed. It is through this entrance that feed and water are carried and cleaning is done. This arrangement for storage and entrance works out great during the blustery cold winter winds. It also cuts down on heat escape and keeps cold winter winds from blowing directly into the henhouse itself. The potting shed area is multipurpose for the birds as well, housing a brooder and a very large dog kennel to be used as needed.

The henhouse, which runs the length of the back of the building, has plywood interior walls from ceiling to floor. A double walled henhouse is warmer, air tight, and mouse proof, let alone predator proof. The dead air space between the walls helps insulate the henhouse against drafts.

Do not insulate an unheated henhouse. The insulation will tend to keep the moisture in rather than the cold out. Moisture is the worse of the two evils, as it can cause respiratory problems. Any loose insulation could make the birds ill should they eat it, and it could be an invitation for mice to make nests in should they gain access to it. One should worry about drafts even more so than the cold.

Caution must be taken when a henhouse is built directly on the ground or with a wire bottom. Fencing and wire must be secure. Predators can dig under the house to get in. A friend of mine built a beautiful portable guinea coop. The floor to the coop was closely woven wire mesh so that droppings fell through to the ground. This building could be pulled to different locations in the yard with the family riding mower. All seemed safe until one morning she went out to find guinea parts scattered all over her yard and the wire floor torn! The one surviving guinea never would return to that coop. Eventually it left in search of a new home. It was later discovered that a neighboring dog was the predator, but not until after the family had started over with new keets. Her brooder, high on legs, the same with wire flooring, was broken into and all keets were once again brutalized. In both cases, the material used was welded wire, and in both cases, the enclosures were broken into over night.

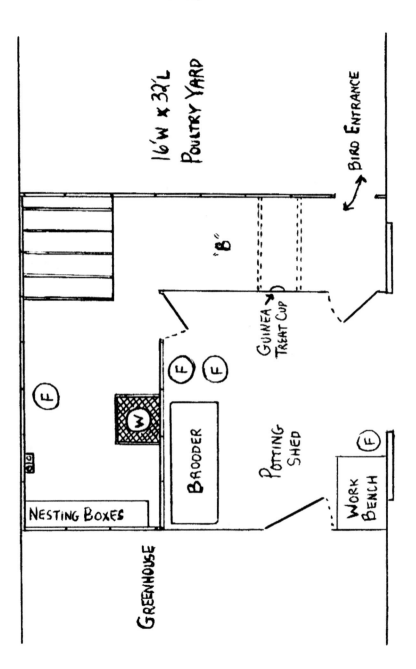

Pictures of the multipurpose building show the entrance to the potting shed. Inside are entrances to the greenhouse and guinea/chicken house.

On the right side is the bird entrance, inside a fenced yard for the chickens. Note the wood along the top of the 6' fence, it is a landing strip for the guineas to use when entering or exiting.

Guineas will occasionally lay eggs in the nesting boxes meant for chickens. If necessary, keeping guineas indoors until noon or so may force them to lay eggs in the henhouse rather than on their hidden nest outside.

Guineas prefer to nest outdoors in natural surroundings, but will return to roost in the henhouse each evening when trained.

As my flock grew in size, Section B was added to the henhouse. Section B adds an extra 10' X 4' area. It is at the front of this area where the birds are able to exit or enter the henhouse. The wall between the potting shed and this section is plywood on the bottom half, with welded wire fencing reaching from half way up to the ceiling just for fun. Two tree branches are at this mid-height for guineas to sit or roost on. (It is too high for the chickens reach) Some of the guineas enjoy looking around from them, as I leave the doors to the potting shed open during good weather, and they are able to see outdoors easily. Between the perches on the welded wire hangs a feed cup, which I sometimes use as a special treat dish for the guineas.

The minimum size of your henhouse depends on the number of birds you plan to keep times the square foot requirement for that particular breed. When *Gardening With Guineas,* keep in mind the guineas will only be in the house to roost overnight, and all day only during extreme weather conditions. A general guideline would be to allow 3 to 4 square feet per guinea. Constant overcrowding causes fighting, pecking and feather pulling.

An experience with a mink gaining entrance to the henhouse convinced us to board the eaves as well as the walls in an attempt to keep out any other possible intruders. Should anything try to eat or dig its way in now, we would surely notice immediately. Although the chickens and guineas would kill any mice that were to get in, I personally do not like them, nor want them running across these toes of mine when I am in there in sandals in the summertime, or in boots in the winter for that matter!

Inside the hen house itself are typical standard galvanized metal nesting boxes for chickens along one end wall. These are the standard commercial, community type having 3 rows of 5 boxes each. Each cubby is about a foot square, open on the front, and hung against a solid wall. Only one cubby is necessary for every 8 hens. Each row of the nesting box has a landing board running the length of the row for jumping onto and easy access to and from the box. Prior to having the commercial boxes, we had built our own nesting boxes from plywood. In either set up, removable bottoms in each box makes cleaning a lot easier! Chickens always lay their eggs in the nesting boxes, however they are not necessary if you will be raising only guinea fowl. If the boxes are filled with loose straw, a guinea might occasionally lay an egg or even make a nest in one, but not very often.

Sometimes the young guinea will sleep on one of these perches or even in a nesting box. However, it is normally on the huge roosts where the chickens and older guineas will share sleeping arrangements.

The roosts should be ladder type. Because of the chickens, mine start about 2' off the ground, and continue nearly to the ceiling at a slant, looking like a ladder for a giant leaning against the wall. Each perch is of 2"X2" wood, with beveled edges making it easier on their feet and for their toes to grab and hang on to.

The first rung stands on framed hinged legs that fold back and up against the "ladder". The top "ladder legs" are on strong hinges. For cleaning purposes, this "ladder" folds back flat against the wall in one easy swinging movement.

When settling in for the night, my guineas prefer the highest of the roosts. Of course, for guineas only, a few perches up high would work just fine, as long as they have room in the hen house to make the jump up to it. In this case, a few tree branches will work nicely. I prefer the ladder method also because it saves on leg injuries that could happen when jumping down in a confined area. In my henhouse, the perches are about 4' wide and 1' apart. Each bird should have approximately 10" to roost on.

Under the roost is the messiest part of the henhouse, so the bedding on the floor is thicker there. Actually, it is the chickens who are the messiest and smelliest ones. Guineas alone in a henhouse would not be bad at all. Their droppings are drier and do not have a strong ammonia odor, as do the chickens. As needed, I shovel the straw into a garden cart that fits through the doorway to the henhouse, then dump it out back on a compost pile for a while before it gets spread on the garden. Cleaning the henhouse floor monthly works for me. Some consider this to be an annual job. However, the guineas need cleaner flooring, as will be discussed in another chapter.

Hanging from the ceiling over mid roost is a hooded heat lamp. During extremely cold winter nights it is turned on for those who need it. Most often, I find my chicken rooster parked under it. He has the prettiest comb you have ever laid eyes on. A rooster exposed to freezing temperatures might get a frost bitten comb that will eventually break off. A guinea feeling poorly will also appreciate the extra warmth from the bulb. A heat lamp does tend to take the chill out of the henhouse as well. Mine is so far above the bedding on the floor that I feel safe allowing it to remain on for long periods of time without the worry of a fire.

Windows provide needed sunshine, light, and ventilation. Ones facing south will allow the most sunshine and light. Mine are screened glass windows that are closed and draft-free in the winter. Winter ventilation is plentiful from the bird sized opening which should continue to be opened each morning with the exception of sub-zero weather.

Fresh water needs to always be available in the henhouse for guineas and chickens. I prefer the three-gallon heavy gauge galvanized steel double wall fountain designed for birds. The top is constructed to prevent roosting, and has a handle for easy carrying. They are available in 2, 3, 5, and 8-gallon containers. Regardless, if the container is empty or not, it is better to change the water each evening. As needed mid day or in the morning, just carry the water outside and tip it to pour out any dirt or straw that may have fallen in.

To help keep the water clean, I built a stand for the water font. This stand is simply a 3' square-shaped frame made using 2X4's standing on edge. I stapled strong 1"X2" welded wire to the top of it, taking care no sharp edges remained loose to cut feet! Dirt or straw from the floor of the henhouse tends to fall through the wire to the bottom of the stand rather than to get into the water. It is amazing how well this works!

Freezing fountains are no fun, and expanding ice can ruin your fountain permanently. For winter protection, use a fountain heater with a built in thermostat that keeps water at 50 to 55 degrees. The element I have is 125 watts and operates only when the temperature drops below 50. The water fountain sits directly on this flat, 16" diameter heater that is about 4" high. The cord on the heater is about 6' long with a ground plug. Needless to say, the heater is for indoor use only. Sit the heater near a sidewall in the henhouse. That way the cord can run up the wall to an outlet high on the wall or on the ceiling. A heater like this can be found in farm supply stores, sometimes at a local feed mill, or in mail order poultry or farm catalogs.

For feed, use a large hanging feeder constructed for birds of all ages. They are of strong galvanized steel with a tray at the bottom the food automatically drops into. This feed container is designed so birds are unable to scratch in it. This container will hold around 40 pounds of feed. How often you fill it will depend on the number of birds you have. Hanging this container from the ceiling by a rope at a height even with that of the youngest bird's back is best. Should your birds begin to toss food out with their beaks and appear to be wasting it, raise the container higher until they cannot or just put enough feed in for a day at a time until they stop. It is preferable to allow guineas to free feed, eating when they are hungry.

One can hang small, galvanized metal rabbit feeders directly on the wall for grit and oyster shell. Both should always be available for chickens and guineas to help themselves to as needed. Supply houses have numerous containers available, some specifically for grit and oyster shell. An alternative to purchasing galvanized equipment is to simply use buckets or plastic containers or whatever you have available that suits your own needs.

Equipment pictured above is commonly used for most poultry. The water stand is excellent for keeping water clean.

In the henhouse should hang a 60-watt bulb. If you have chickens, this light can be set to provide additional light to total 14 hours so they continue to lay eggs well throughout the winter days of shortened sunlight. Although additional light is not necessary for guinea fowl who do not lay eggs in the winter, this light can add brightness to an otherwise gloomy henhouse on a dark winter day. The perfect solution would be to combine a light detector with a timer. Fluorescent lighting could be used in place of the 60-watt bulb, however, in cold weather fluorescent lighting sometimes has a problem starting. In the winter, you can use outdoor bulbs, which last longer in the cold. In my potting shed is a 15-watt bulb I like to keep on at all times for my own benefit. I enjoy having a small nightlight in there. It also casts light to the bird's private door helping them see their way in at night should I miss the evening routine and they get side tracked.

Also in the henhouse should be a private "nursery area" which is discussed in Chapter Four. Mine is simply a fenced section under the nesting boxes for new birds. The fencing should be closely woven wire as keets are able to fit right through chicken wire. A section of the fence should be framed to allow removal for easy cleaning of the nursery area. It would be easiest to have the nursery the length of the nesting boxes and flush with the front of them.

Covering the floor of the henhouse should be an absorbent material such as hay, straw, or wood shavings. I prefer a light straw layer on the wood floor, but heavier under the roosts. Cleaning more often is easier than waiting and having to shovel and lift heavily soiled litter. Dry litter encourages the flock to move around when enclosed due to weather extremes.

Wood shavings, such as used for horse stalls, are drier and better to use if one is not willing to clean the henhouse frequently. Course wood shavings should be laid to a depth of about 8 inches and can be raked over once every couple of weeks. Providing the litter is kept dry, bacterial action breaks down all wastes keeping the pen fresh. The secret is to keep the litter dry. Kept this way, your birds would possibly be able to go through the winter with maybe only one litter change. So long as the litter is still reasonably fresh, all you may need to do is top it up with some fresh shavings and do no more.

Soggy, wet straw is asking for trouble. It encourages insect pests like mites. Due to its retention of moisture, it can greatly increase the incidence of coccidiosis. Straw does not absorb moisture as well as wood shavings. Wet straw creates a high risk of molds that can result in respiratory diseases in both birds and humans. Watch for leaky water containers. When choosing a material for a floor covering, the determining factors are which birds will be housed in the coop, and how often it will be cleaned. Keep in mind the fact that guineas produce a dryer dropping than chickens, and when housed alone, straw should be no problem as long as it is kept dry.

Chickens and guineas should have an opening sized just for them to go from their hen house into the yard. My opening is at henhouse floor level, and has a vertical sliding door. I simply raise the door, and prop it open with a 2"X2" board the height of the opening (to the side so it cannot be knocked over). It closes easily from either the outside or inside of the hen house, which is extremely beneficial. A plank to walk on from the height of the floor down to the yard itself is helpful for the birds and easier on their legs and feet as well. Use small cross boards on the plank to prevent slipping when it is wet from rain or snow. A ladder type plank could be used instead.

THE YARD

The mini door in my henhouse opens to a chicken yard enclosed with 6' high welded wire fencing. The top of the yard is not fenced. The 6' fencing is held in place by 8 1/2'X4"X4" placed posts sunk 2 1/2 feet into the ground so as not to shift during the winter freeze and thaws. Surrounding the bottom of the yard by the fencing are rods sunk deep enough into ground and close enough together to prevent digging into the yard by a predator. Around the top edge are 2X4's for the guineas to land on when flying in or out of the yard. The top of the fencing is attached to this wood for extra strength.

The top of the yard is completely open. Keep in mind the yard needs to be big enough so that the guinea has room to fly up to the landing board or back into the yard from it. When raising both chickens and guineas, I have found this open yard method to work quite well for both the guineas and myself.

The yard should have a shaded area if the building itself does not provide shade. Grassy areas are nice, however chickens will eat every blade as it grows leaving the yard bare. Ideally, to be able to rotate yards is highly desirable for both the prevention of worms and to be able to keep grassy patches growing in the pen. In my yard there is a tree stump for chickens and guineas to have something to jump up on. In a corner is a tree branch sticking through the fencing on each side about 1 1/2' off the ground for daytime outdoor roosting if desired.

A human entrance gate to the yard is a big plus. It can be used to walk the birds in early if needed. Stepping-stones from the human entrance gate to their door can provide easy access in muddy weather. The yard itself can be basically maintenance free, as rain water cleans it, and the chickens make sure there is no grass to trim away from the fencing.

A yard is not necessary for guineas alone. However, it is nice to have for the safety of an injured guinea who is unable to fly until it recovers since it can still be outdoors safely. A yard is also nice since it protects young guineas who have not yet discovered how to fly out and free range.

ALTERNATIVE HOUSING

Housing in warmer climates may be open-front, similar to a henhouse, with secure fencing on one of the four sides. This type of building will offer a dry shelter and wind protection from extreme weather conditions as well as safety from predators if guineas are confined overnight.

Outdoor roosts hung under the eave of a henhouse or barn is another option. No safer than a tree, it is in fact, perhaps less safe because there is no added coverage from branches or leaves.

Trees? Yes, roosting in trees and living wild is an option. When roosting in a tree overnight, chances are guineas will become dinner for an owl or other predator if they survive the temperature extremes and are able to find food and water year around. Also, if the guineas are raised to be wild, they will have no true sense of home and most likely will eventually just leave.

One night on another man's farm where guineas were permitted to roost in trees, strong winds blew his birds from the cedar trees to the snow below. The wind chill factor was tremendous and drifting snow was covering the nearly frozen guineas. He put those he could find under a heat lamp in his barn, but it was too late. Many of his birds had frozen helmets, wattles or frozen toes. Some of the birds survived, but eventually the parts that had been frozen fell off, leaving those birds with stumps and other deformities. Some lost the outer layers of their beaks. Others lost their toes or part of them. One guinea even lost part of his leg.

Another friend insisted roosting in trees was just fine. Her guineas roosted in a particular tree every night, and she was happy by not having to maintain chores. One morning she went outdoors and found guinea parts all over the place. Some parts were still hanging from the trees. Every single bird had been killed overnight. She now has a beautiful henhouse and has started over, beginning with eggs.

Ultimately, the type of housing selected will be the determining factor in raising wild or tamed guinea fowl. My goal is to have domesticated free-ranging, yet trained, guinea fowl that protect my property by day, that have the desire to stay on my property and not leave for greener pastures, and who will return each night to their henhouse for safety. Guinea Fowl are my organic gardeners who eat the bugs, insects and weed seeds for me without the use of chemicals. I raise guinea fowl for *Gardening With Guineas*.

3 *Which Comes First, The Guinea or the Egg?*

OLDER GUINEAS

Some may inherit their guineas by moving to a farm where the owners moved away, but guineas remained. Perhaps one or a pair has wandered in from an unhappy home. It is possible someone has a few extras to "give away" and it is just too tempting to say no. A guinea in a pen at the fair is just "SO CUTE" with a desirable price tag to match? Maybe a few which appear to be healthy and have feathers already are spotted in a barn sale or during chick days at the local farm and feed store! Maybe a neighbor or friend is moving and offers free guineas to a good home?

It is hard to train an old guinea, just as it is to teach an old dog new tricks. Guineas are wild by nature, somewhat difficult to handle, and they frighten easily. To raise a guinea who will permit touching and taming, one should begin with day old keets. Although starting with older birds is not totally impossible, training is harder and by far less successful.

DAY OLD KEETS

Sources for day old keets are not too difficult to locate. My preference is to find a local breeder. The local feed mill is a great source for information. Most have bulletin boards where farmers post notices of straw, hay, and animals for sale. Some feed mills have what they call "chick day" and order in a large number of chicks once a year for resale. Sometimes they are able to get a few keets. If there is no bulletin board, the employees will most likely know just who sells what in an area based on the feed purchased by certain regular customers or by word of mouth. The newspaper might also list a local breeder under agriculture or farm animals for sale.

A trip to the poultry barn during a county fair is a sure way to spot a local breeder. If guineas are not found, just ask around. Surely the 4H leader or one of the poultry owners will know of a local source for guinea fowl in the area if there is one.

When purchasing keets from a local, not only is it possible to see the adult guineas, and perhaps see the setup and cleanliness on that particular farm, it is also possible to be able to purchase the exact number of keets desired. A proud owner and good caretaker will be more than happy to show someone around the homestead.

When making a purchase locally, take along a normal shoe box in which to carry the keets home. Keets are very tiny. A normal sized shoebox can easily transport up to twenty, day-old, keets. A bit of shredded straw in the bottom will keep them from sliding around in the box during the ride home. The lid will help keep in body heat; air holes are not necessary for a short trip. Most important, keep them warm! Air conditioning in the car or open drafty windows during the ride home are a no-no. If keets chill, they may very well become ill. Keeping the box next to the driver or on the lap of a passenger allows for checking on the keets, which also lets in a bit of fresh air.

Mail order is always an option. Hatcheries are available all over the United States, and the larger ones normally advertise day old keets during season. Mail order is the easiest way to find a particular color of guinea. Mail order is also the easiest way to receive the keets at a time most convenient for the homeowner to care for them. I was happy with my order of thirty keets from a certain hatchery which two local residents and myself divided. We picked them up at the local post office at 7AM the day after they were shipped from the hatchery.

There are a few drawbacks to mail order. It is common to find a minimum requirement of twenty-five to thirty keets per order. Hatcheries have legitimate reasons for selling keets in large quantities. Keets in transit are dependent upon the body heat from each other to survive without a heat lamp during shipment. They huddle closely together during travel; it is possible for the one in the center to smother. The keets go without water or food, which is common for any newborn keet to do the first few hours of life. However, normal shipment is overnight, at times two or more days depending on how far the keets will travel. In most cases though, the keets arrive overnight and can be picked up at a post office in the early AM by the buyer. There may be one or two dead birds upon arrival or sick ones who die within a few days. A decent hatchery is fair about refunding money for any dead keets, but cannot replace them due to the need to ship another twenty-five or thirty at a time. Some hatcheries will include an extra keet in the order, just in case. If you receive birds with a few feathers, they are not day old.

The number of keets to begin with is totally up to an individual, keeping in mind the size of the adult housing and dependant on the location and size of the property. My suggestion is to begin with twice the number one wants to keep. I have often convinced those who want only a pair to begin with a minimum of four to six. The guinea fowl are happier in groups. Unfortunately, most who are new to raising guineas will lose a few the first year for various reasons.

THE EGG AND EGG CARE

My ultimate preference and the way I actually started myself, was to begin with the egg. An incubator with a fully transparent lid permits the best view when watching the entire process! The thrill of caring for the egg, remaining glued to the incubator during the hatch and watching the miracle of birth is something I look forward to each year. Giving the keet its first drink of water and being a vital part of the keets existence creates a bond with the flock and a strong sense of responsibility toward the life of one's birds. Raising keets from eggs is quite an education and learning experience for any child.

Eggs are available during season by mail order in some poultry catalogs. With excellent care a 90% hatch rate can be expected. However, not even a hatchery will guarantee that eggs purchased will be 100% fertile. Guinea eggs are smaller and thicker shelled than chicken eggs, and nearly impossible to candle for fertility until they are 10 days into incubation. If purchasing eggs from a local source, select eggs for hatching that are from mature, healthy guineas. Take notice of crippled toes, a sign of too much in-breeding. Choose clean eggs if possible. I have successfully hatched eggs that were slightly dirty with no problem, but would not put a filthy egg in my incubator. Do not wash or wipe dirty eggs. The shell is porous. To try to clean an egg or rub it clean could force possible disease organisms into the egg itself. Cracked or punctured shells have difficulty retaining the moisture needed for proper keet development. Proper care of the eggs by both the seller and consumer is necessary for a good hatch.

Scrambled eggs will not hatch. Do handle the egg with care so as not to disturb any part of it. The germ spot is the small, tough white spot in the egg, always attached to the egg yolk. (Germ spots are visible in store bought eggs too.) The yolk and egg whites are inside thin, transparent membranes. An air pocket at the large end of the egg is filled with oxygen. The shell has thousands of tiny holes that are impossible to see, allowing the egg to breathe.

It is the germ spot in a fertile egg that becomes the keet. Before the egg is hatched, the keet is called an embryo. The embryo gets nourishment from the egg yolk. The egg white surrounds the embryo and cushions the shock between the embryo and the shell so it is protected when bumped or moved.

Eggs must be gathered daily for food consumption. However, to gather the eggs daily for hatching is not the norm for a breeder. A good guinea hen will lay an egg a day in a secluded nest. If the eggs are removed, she will most likely make a nest elsewhere. If all but four to six eggs are removed from a nest for safekeeping, she may return to the same spot and continue laying. In most cases, a dozen eggs purchased from a guinea farmer will come from a find of one nest having several eggs in it. Keep in mind, the guinea hen lays an egg a day and normally will go broody when the nest has around thirty eggs in the clutch. Therefore, the eggs from a local will most likely vary from a day to a three weeks old or more already! These eggs should be placed into incubation immediately.

Eggs from confined guineas can be collected daily with no problem. When purchasing from a hatchery, most likely those eggs can be kept for a few days before beginning incubation if needed. Keep in mind the possible number of days the eggs were in transit, and adjust accordingly.

The embryo does begin to develop prior to the incubation period, and proper management of undeveloped eggs is as just as important as the incubation period itself. Rough handling can ruin fertile eggs. Eggs should be stored in an egg carton with the smaller and more pointed end facing downward. The ideal room temperature for storing the eggs is 55 degrees. A cool basement works well, however do not refrigerate fertile eggs to be hatched. (Yes, it is possible for some refrigerated eggs to hatch, however I recommend against it for a higher hatch rate.) Eggs stored for several days need to be turned once daily to prevent the yolk from sticking to the inside of the shell. Storing eggs for more than 10 days reduces the hatch rate drastically. A clutch of thirty eggs should be incubated immediately with no holding period.

INCUBATION

There are three ways to hatch the guinea eggs. Allowing a guinea hen to hatch her own clutch is discussed later in this book. Other options are to use a chicken surrogate or an incubator.

A CHICKEN SURROGATE

One option for hatching is to put the guinea eggs under a broody hen. A good broody hen will remain on the nest after the normal 21-day period it takes to hatch her chicks. Take care not to place more than she can actually cover. Twenty guinea eggs is an approximate number for most hens to be able to handle. However, the number of eggs a hen can hatch will be dependent on the breed and size of chicken. By placing the eggs in an empty nesting box, usually a good broody chicken hen will find them and take over.

Once I had a guinea who made her nest in one of the nesting boxes in the henhouse. Daily, the nest gained an egg, sometimes two, because guinea hens will often share a nest. I was most curious to observe the entire process, so I watched and waited. Eventually, having counted forty plus eggs in that nest (beginning to wonder I might add) that guinea hen went broody in there. She fluffed herself out and covered all of those eggs with no problem. It seemed she never got off the nest, as least not when I went in to check. About fifteen days later, I noticed she had gotten off that nest. I was really worried the eggs might have gotten cold, not knowing how long she had been off them. I forced myself to let that nest go untouched by my hands, as I wanted to learn the outcome. Later that day, I went in to find a Rhode Island Red had gone broody on the same nest. I sensed trouble when the guinea hen returned, but that was not the case. The next morning, to my amazement, I found both the Rhode Island Red hen and the guinea hen together, broody on the same nest inside of that one foot square nesting box. They were there, side by side, both facing the front opening, just looking at me as if to say "What is your problem?" It was really something else to see the two together!

This arrangement continued for the next week or so until one day the guinea hen decided she had had enough. The Rhode Island Red continued to fluff herself out over those forty some guinea eggs. Right on time, at what I had recorded to be the hatch date, I went in to find the hen squirming over thirty-three keets! Well, it was so obvious she did not have enough room to sit, so I moved her and her babies to a dog kennel I prepared in the potting shed. In the kennel, the hen continued to be the best mother. She taught the keets to drink and eat, and kept them warm under her wings.

Another time I had a Rhode Island Red successfully hatch nearly twenty keets. Most were spoken for, and she was obviously upset when I removed them once they had dried. However, I allowed her to keep two keets and raise them as her own. What an experience this was! When she took them outdoors for the first time, one disappeared, but the other remained with her like glue. "Chickeeta" as I named her, was one of a kind. Each night Chickeeta would roost snuggled under the wing of her mother. It was a sight for sore eyes to see all the guineas, chickens, and roosters perched on the roosts in my henhouse, and Chickeeta there under mamma's wing. As she grew and became larger than dear old mom, Chickeeta still wanted to cuddle. To see mom with her wing stretched out around this speckled plump-bodied bird was just too funny.

Eventually, during mating season of the following spring, Chickeeta discovered she could fly like the other guineas, and began flying up to the landing strip atop the fenced yard. However, that is all she would do, keeping her mamma in site every second. Mother chicken would seem to be communicating with Chickeeta. I only wish I knew what she was saying. In time, Chickeeta decided to check out life on the other side of the fence, and discovered a more desirable diet, room to roam, and that the grass really is greener on the other side of the fence.

It wasn't too long before Chickeeta joined the rest of the guineas and ranged with them, soon to become one of the flock, the other guineas accepting her from day one with no problems. Finding her own identity took months. She was the tamest of all guineas as she thought herself a chicken all along since she had been treated as one. She was held and petted by the children and me often, receiving special treatment and more attention than most of the "other chickens". As time passed and she grew, there was never a doubt as to which guinea was Chickeeta amongst the crowd. If a chicken hen successfully hatches keets, it is an option to allow her to raise them in the same manner as she would raise chicks. She will teach them to drink and eat. Most chickens are excellent mothers.

THE INCUBATOR

Use of an incubator to hatch guinea eggs is my choice since it produces the most success of any method I have tried. However, there is more to incubating the eggs than just plugging in the incubator, sticking in a few eggs and waiting.

If the incubator is not brand new, it will need to be thoroughly cleaned. Scrub with detergent, then rinse using an anti-bacterial rinse or a bit of bleach mixed with water. Follow this by a thorough rinsing with clean water. Residue left from the cleansers could harm the new keets or contaminate the eggs.

The incubator should be placed indoors. This way outdoor temperature changes and weather are not as likely to affect the uniform temperature and humidity inside the incubator itself. When indoors, it is much easier to keep an eye on the temperature, to maintain the humidity level by keeping the water reservoirs filled, and to turn the eggs after the incubation begins. Year after year my incubator has sat on an extra dining room chair against the wall. This way it is at a level easy to watch and convenient to care for. There is no smell to a clean incubator or to the hatch itself. The incubator is clean and the hatch is not messy. Only a rotten egg, incubated after a number of days, produces a horrible odor. In that case, to remove and dispose of a rotten egg is simple enough

Determine where the incubator will be located permanently until after the hatch. It should not be placed in a draft or where wind from a window or fan will blow on it because the embryo can develop pneumonia easily. Too much heat from being near a furnace vent or direct sunlight can kill an embryo as can carbon dioxide from a gas heater. The ideal location would be a room in a house around 72 degrees, away from either a window or heater. Put the incubator in place, make certain it is level, and then plug it in. Always read the information that comes with an incubator and follow the manufacturer's directions as they can vary from one type of incubator to another.

Mine is a forced-air incubator with a fan to provide internal air circulation. The fan also pulls fresh air from the room through very tiny air holes near the fan motor hung from the center of the lid. The correct temperature for guinea eggs is 99 1/2 degrees, to be maintained throughout the entire hatch.

Ventilation is extremely important. During the development of the embryo, oxygen enters and carbon dioxide escapes the egg through the shell. As embryos grow, keep the plugged air vent openings closed on top of an air-circulating incubator. Enough fresh air is pulled in through the openings for the fan. Air circulates completely around the eggs since they sit on a wire mesh and not directly on the bottom of the incubator itself. Excellent ventilation and air movement is provided in an air-circulating incubator.

A special incubator thermometer is necessary to be able to monitor the inside temperature. Incubator thermometers are made so that the bulb of the thermometer sits at the level of the egg laying on its side. If the eggs are placed vertically on a self-turning incubator, the bulb should be placed 1/4 to 1/2 inch below the top of the eggs. This places the bulb of the thermometer at the level of the developing embryo. Do not allow the thermometer to touch the egg, or the result will be an incorrect reading. Higher temperatures will result in an earlier hatch with fewer keets. Colder temperatures will result in a later hatch, also with fewer keets.

Also available is a still-air incubator. These do not have fans for air circulation. Temperature should be maintained at 102 degrees in a still-air incubator. In this type incubator, the bulb of the thermometer should be even with the top of the eggs. Due to layering of the warmth in these types of incubators, the temperature maintained around the egg is not always uniform, but it is still adequate for incubation.

Make sure you maintain the water level in the water reservoir built into the incubator for necessary humidity. The most important factors in a successful hatch are maintenance of the humidity level and temperature, as well proper turning of the eggs. Always fill the water trays with warm, not cold tap water to avoid extreme temperature changes in the incubator caused by adding cold water. The water should be under the mesh screen the eggs sit on so that when the keets hatch they will not be able to fall in water and drown. Some incubators come with a hydrometer to measure the humidity. Read the instructions that came with the incubator on how to maintain the humidity and to be certain of the location of the water reservoirs.

Once the incubator has been in place, plugged in and running for a few days with temperatures monitored and humidity maintained, allow the stored eggs to come to room temperature. Freshly collected eggs need to come to room temperature also before being placed directly in an incubator. Shocking a cold egg by placing it directly in the incubator not only risks harming the germ cell of the egg itself, but can cause moisture condensation on the egg shell that could lead to reduced hatch rates.

I always time the hatch to begin at a time when the children will be here to enjoy the miracle. Counting backward twenty-eight days from a Monday or Sunday is simple enough to plan for the hatch to take place on a weekend.

Guinea eggs are smaller than chicken eggs. Guinea eggs weigh about 1.4 ounces each while chicken eggs average about 2 ounces each. The size of the incubator will determine the number of eggs that will fit in it. Please read the directions that come with the incubator to determine the number of eggs that will fit properly.

Once the eggs are room temperature, it is safe to add them. Fingers should be clean. Oil from fingers can soil the shell, enter the egg, and cause reduced hatching. Using a pencil, place a small x about midway on one side of the egg and place the pencil mark face up in the incubator. Do not use marker or ink which could penetrate the shell. For easy turning, it is nice to place an equal number of eggs in rows pointing in the same direction. Although not necessary, this works best for me. Take care to handle the eggs with caution while turning. Severely handling, shaking, or dropping an egg could kill the embryo by rupturing the delicate blood vessels inside the egg. Be careful when there is a large number of eggs, it is easy to bump one not yet turned and it could roll.

Once the incubation period has begun, do not add more guinea eggs. However, on day seven you could successfully add a few chicken eggs after allowing them to warm to room temperature. Correct timing will cause all eggs in the incubator to "be due" on the same date. Chicken eggs take twenty-one days to hatch, guinea eggs take twenty-six to twenty-eight days. Keep in mind this will alter the temperature inside the incubator while the chicken eggs heat up to the 99 1/2 degree temp inside the incubator, and possibly reduce the number of keets that will hatch.

Guinea eggs need to be turned at least five times daily. More is better than less. I turn the eggs more often because the incubator is conveniently placed inside my house. The first thing in the morning and last at night, as well as spaced intervals throughout the day is best. When turning the eggs, lift the lid slightly with one hand while reaching inside the incubator with the other. Quickly, but carefully, turn each egg one at a time placing the penciled x downward. The next turn, the x will be back on top. This way there is no doubt as to possibly forgetting to turn an egg.

Do you wonder why it is necessary to turn the egg? The yolk has a tendency to float toward the shell. If the egg were to lie too long in one position, the white could separate and allow the yolk to float through. This would force the germ against the shell and kill it. When the egg is turned, the embryo also gets exercise because it will turn inside the shell until its head is upright.

Some of the larger incubators come with automatic turners; however, I have not had the experience of using one of these. I normally hatch up to fifty eggs at a time without the use of an automatic turner without problems. An automatic turner actually tilts the eggs from side to side every so many hours rather than to actually turn them. Eggs are placed in the holders on end, with the more pointed end down. Reading the manufacturer's advice and the instructions that come with each incubator is necessary to learn how to operate your particular incubator entirely.

Be certain the humidity level is maintained by water in the reservoir during the entire incubation period, or the keet can dry off before it gets out of the shell and actually stick to it. The moisture in the incubator keeps the natural moisture in the egg from drying out.

Beginning on day 23, turning the eggs is not necessary. At this time the keets are moving into hatching position. Keep the lid closed on the incubator during this time to maintain proper temperature and humidity. In the wintertime with the additional dryness in the air, keep the water reservoirs filled to capacity during the final days of the hatch. If day 23 falls during the spring or summer, the extra humidity needed at this time may be provided from the hatching keets themselves while drying off.

Day 26, the hatch begins.

4 *The Birds Are Coming! Now What?*

THE INCUBATOR HATCH HAS BEGUN!

The keets will begin pipping on day twenty-six of the hatch. Pipping is the correct term to use for breaking out of the shell. At first a very tiny pinhole will be noticed, sometimes in the center of what appears to be a light colored circular thin spot on the shell. Then a tiny piece of shell will fall off. Soon the beak tooth will be seen pipping at the shell. Eventually a somewhat jagged yet nearly straight line will be pipped around the shell, always toward the large end of the egg. Sometimes chirping can be heard from within the egg even before pipping is seen.

At times, it may seem the keet has died or is in trouble. Keep in mind, it can take from a half-hour to 2 full days for a keet to hatch! Do not help. The keet will work a while, then nap or sleep a while. If a keet cannot get out, assume it was not meant to be. Often times, that keet will either be deformed, a runt, or simply be extremely weak and would not have survived long anyway. I have aided keets, only to later wish I did not. Given time, most will hatch on their own. Perhaps the keet will be stuck to the shell, and helping it hatch will result in pulling off part of the fur, a piece of skin, etc., causing the keet to nearly bleed to death. To see an egg rolling around in the incubator is not unusual. It is simply the keet changing positions, and does not necessarily mean it is in a life-threatening situation. Sit back, relax, and enjoy the miracle of birth right before your eyes.

When the first keet has hatched, remove the vent plugs on the incubator to increase the supply of fresh oxygen and proper air exchange needed by both the newly hatched keets and the embryos yet to hatch. Tempting as it may be, it is not necessary to help the wet keet or to remove the shell immediately. Opening the lid will let in a rush of cold air. Wait until the keet is fully dry before handling it, which could take an hour or longer. Meanwhile, prepare the brooder.

There is no need to lose sleep over worry of not being present during a hatch. The keets will often hatch while I am fast asleep, or not home with them. Although I prefer to remove a newly hatched keet within a few hours, it can survive longer. (I am not willing to find out exactly how long.)

Once the keet is fully dry and active, reach in and lift it out gently, replacing the lid quickly for other keets may be drying, hatching, or pipping yet! Move the keet to a prepared brooder. The egg shell can be removed at the same time.

Hatchings will continue through day twenty-eight. If proper temperatures were not maintained, it is possible a keet might hatch a day or two after that, but not often.

Checking unhatched eggs out of curiosity will sometimes aid future hatches, by determining the problems encountered - marked by the age of an underdeveloped fetus or none at all. This should be done outside of course, due to the stench of an overcooked egg or dead embryo.

The worse scenario is to have a power outage during a hatch. This is one of those situations when an auxiliary generator would certainly come in handy! However the small farmer and those of us raising a few guineas and keets to be gardeners do not normally own that equipment. In the case of a power outage with no generator, open the lid of the incubator to let in fresh air until the power returns. Depending on the room temperature, use your best judgment to either open the lid (or door) a little or remove the lid entirely. A hot stuffy location is worse than a cooler, well-ventilated one. Some keets may not survive from the cool down, but with a closed lid, all could be lost from the lack of oxygen.

Never say never. This happened to me in 1998 for the first time. The time was early spring when the weather was cold yet, and the furnace was still running. The power was out for nearly six hours, and the house cooled down rather quickly. Unfortunately, the day the power went out was day twenty-six of the hatch. Some had already hatched while others were pipping. With no generator, I had to think fast. Well, I put the wet keet against my body in a soft tissue tucked in my bra. Say what you will, that keet lived! I then put the incubator with lid ajar in the back of my car, a blazer, and parked it the sun. It was warmer there than in the house, and had plenty of fresh air. Sun always seems to heat a car nicely. I could have put them in the greenhouse, but thought if it were to be longer, at least I had the car engine and heater in the vehicle to turn on if necessary, or would drive them to a friends house who did have power. But, as it turned out, the power outage lasted only about six hours. When day twenty-eight arrived, my hatch rate was 95%. Of the remaining eggs, one was dead and the rest were not fertile.

The keets in this incubator have not yet fully dried.

THE BROODER

The first home for a new keet is simply a brooder in the form of a cardboard box. Get a clean one from the grocery store that is at least about 2' x 1' and a 1' deep. Although straw, untreated wood chips, shavings or other bedding materials may be used, I prefer to layer paper towels on newspaper because in the house it is easier, less messy, and easy to change several times daily as needed. Keep the paper or bedding clean, as proper sanitation is important.

The brooder box is not moved around while the keets are in it, so there is no threat of leg injury as there is during shipping when the keets could slide around with nothing to grip onto.

At one end of the box hang a 25 or 40 watt bulb about six inches or higher above the indoor brooder. By using a metal bulb shade available from any hardware or home improvement store, the heat from the lamp is directed to the area below the hood and warms the brooder. The keets will be able to move to the opposite end of the box to get away from the heat source if they get too warm. Some shades come with clamps attached. I clamp the heat lamp to the leg of the chair. My brooder is on the floor next to the incubator...very handy.

Care must be taken to monitor the temperature of the brooder below the lamp. Although the keets hatch in 99 1/2 degrees, the temperature on the floor of the brooder beneath the light should be 95 degrees. Use a thermometer to be certain. If the temperature on the floor of the brooder beneath the light is less than 95 degrees, lower the light. If the temperature on the floor of the brooder beneath the light is above 95 degrees, raise the light.

Place a water container on the opposite side of the box from the lamp for the keets. Although a lid will work at first, I go ahead and get them used to the inverted mason jar with screw-on chick water dish. Available in feed mills or farm stores, these screw-on lids cost fewer than two dollars and work great! Either way, fill the bottom of the water dish with gravel or marbles at first, for the tiny keets can drown in water even this shallow.

NEWBORN AND VERY YOUNG KEETS

Keets, just like human babies, require warmth, fresh water, nutritious protein-rich food, a place to sleep, light, room to play, attention, and lots of tender loving care.

After the keets are born and are fully dry, they need to be placed in this pre-heated cardboard brooder. After lifting each from the incubator, carefully dip the end of its beak in the water to give it its first drink. After a second dip, place the keet directly under the lamp. Do the same for each and every keet that is placed into the brooder, whether it is from mail order, another farm, or hatched in your own incubator.

Keets will eat almost immediately upon being placed in the brooder. Sprinkle their first food on a paper towel near the water and they will peck at it instinctively. However, after the first day, use an automatic feeder for the keets. Also available from the same source that carries the mason lid for water, is a mason lid for chick feed. Using a feeder keeps the feed clean and the keets from walking in it. It is a good idea to keep the jars full so they always have food and water in front of them. All of my birds free-feed, meaning food is always available for them to eat as they want it.

While in the brooder, it is easy to observe that if the keets huddle extremely close, they are too cold. If spread far apart, they are too hot. Keep an eye on the temperature, and raise the lamp higher or lower to adjust the temperature directly under it.

Decide which of the keets you intend to keep, and handle those several times daily beginning now to tame them. Once a day per bird is NOT enough. A tamed keet will sit on your arm, hand, leg, shoulder, and eventually perch on your finger just like a parakeet. Training at this age is imperative if you desire to have tamed adults who will allow you to pet them, pick them up, even come to you on their own for attention. Extremely tame adult guineas will fly to a person's shoulder to be petted! All of this is possible, but only if taming is started immediately after birth.

When the keets turn a week old, lower the temperature in the brooder by 5 degrees. For about two weeks the keets can live in this box. By the third week the keets will be jumping out of the box. One could put a screen over the top of the box temporarily, however it is time for a move to a larger brooder with more room to play when jumping begins.

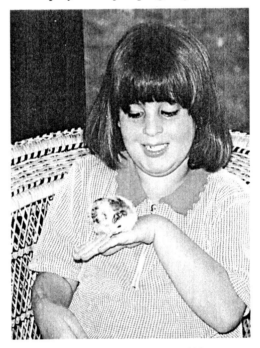

Begin handling keets as soon as possible to tame them.

AGES TWO - SIX WEEKS OLD

The brooder in my potting shed is huge. It stands on legs at a height comfortable for me. The bottom of the brooder stands about 3' off the ground. The brooder box itself is 6' long, 3' wide and 1 1/2' deep. The top of the brooder has a lid on hinges. The framed brooder has 1/4" welded wire for the bottom, top, and four sides, but is also lined with removable plywood for cooler weather. The brooder is partitioned in half with a plywood removable wall, which allows a small area for the very young

keets. The half the young keets go into h
safety. The heat lamp hangs in the cente
    Two to four inches of litter sho'
brooder. Many types are available. Tł
not too expensive, absorbs moisture wɔ..
and dust. Wood shavings purchased in bags ⅄.
work very nicely on the brooder floor, and makes for a ɤ
bedding. Wet litter must be replaced with fresh as needed. Keeɩ₅
that were handled several times daily will be calm when the lid is
opened to change the water and feed.

As the keets grow and need more space, I remove the
divider in the center of the brooder to double the size to the full
6' length. By this time, their tender feet have grown to a size safe
to walk on the half with wire flooring without worry of injury. In
here the keets have plenty of room to play in until they are fully
feathered. Depending on the weather at the time, I use either a
60-watt bulb or a regular heat lamp with a reflector hood. At this
time, I also switch to larger feeders and a larger water font as the
keets eat and drink like little piggies! A one-gallon plastic drop
waterer is nice for the brooder, as is a 20"chick feeder. A chick
feeder of this type permits many to eat at the same time, has a
reel on top to prevent roosting or scratching, and will hold about
five pounds of food. A tree branch or perch across the width of
one end of the brooder, a few inches off the floor, will give the
keets something to roost on, or play on for exercise. The
temperature should be lowered by five degrees weekly by raising
the heat lamp, until the keets are fully feathered. By six weeks of
age the keets will be roosting if a perch is available.

Depending on the set up one has, it is possible for the keets
to move directly to the henhouse or adult home instead of being
in a large brooder. It is important that the keets have access to the
correct temperatures, water and feed. They need to be held in
confinement either in a brooder area inside the henhouse or in a
makeshift "nursery" inside the henhouse. Either way, they should
be able to see everything in the henhouse yet be separated from
the other birds only by fencing during this confinement period.

dless to say, if it is summertime and the weather
s a steady 80 degrees, and the keets are still in a brooder
lower heat requirements, an early move to the henhouse
sery is appropriate. If at the end of six weeks the keet
ecomes fully feathered, but the outdoor temperature is less than
65 degrees, it would be a good idea to provide an optional heat
source for the keets in the henhouse on really cold days or nights
until they are older. I make it a point not to hatch keets after the
first of September so that they are fully feathered before winter
sets in.

Sanitize the brooder between uses. Scrubbing with a mild
solution of bleach and water will kill any bacteria or germs that
could affect the next group of keets. Make sure to rinse well after
scrubbing.

THE NURSERY 6 WEEKS AND UP

I raise enough chickens to provide eggs for the family and a
few friends, not to maintain an egg business. My henhouse is
large enough for my purpose. However, it is not huge. So, under
the nesting boxes mentioned in an earlier chapter, is a removable
framed chicken wire partition. It slides into place easily when
needed. The partition is the full width of the henhouse, and about
1 1/2' high. The bottom of the nesting boxes provides the roof for
the "nursery". A heat lamp is supplied for keets if it is late in the
season and temperatures are a lot colder than the brooder from
which they came.

While in the nursery, new arrivals are able to see the huge
chickens, older guineas and roosters through the fencing, yet are
protected from both a major pecking order and are confined from
exiting the henhouse. It is during the time spent in the "nursery"
that the guineas learn the most important lesson of all. While in
the nursery they learn that the henhouse is home, a place where
they are protected, warm, dry, have a constant supply of feed,
grit, oyster shell, have access to fresh clean water, and feel safe
and secure.

New additions to the flock need to be confined inside the henhouse for a total of six weeks, regardless of the age of the bird(s). A young guinea over 6 weeks or an adult new to the flock could be put directly in the henhouse without being held in confinement. However, when released, it would most likely disappear in search of the home it came from as soon as the door is opened for the other guineas to range. Untrained, it will be a huge struggle to get an unconditioned guinea to go back into the henhouse.

Keets can be calm, and tamed if held frequently.

CAGES AND DOG KENNELS

Large cages can come in handy when a temporary place inside the henhouse is needed to separate an injured bird or to confine an older bird or two that are new to the flock.

Dog kennels are perfect when more privacy is needed. I keep a dog kennel sitting on an old table in the potting shed as a makeshift hospital or nursery, whichever the need might be. The tough plastic kennels are easy to clean and provide privacy for the birds inside. Vents on each side as well as a nice chrome door on the front provides visibility for both the bird and myself as well as great protection for the birds enclosed. Having a dog kennel is not a necessity, but is something that can come in handy for all kinds of animals at various times on a homestead.

Regular cups or dishes such as those used to hang parrot food and water inside a cage work well in the kennel. They will hang on the inside of the metal door and are easy to see for cleaning and refilling the food and water as needed.

FEEDING

Fresh, clean water should always be available, warmed to room temperature for the first few days for newborn keets. Marbles or gravel in the water dish will keep them from falling in and drowning. They will drink from between the marbles.

As soon as the keets are moved to the brooder, start them on turkey starter or starter/grower that contains an anticoccidial medication. The medicated feed I use contains Amprolium, a coccidiostat that controls coccidiosis. I have had no problems with coccidiosis or ill keets when using this medicated feed. Some medicated feed may contain additional antibiotics, which may not be recommended by some. Availability of feed varies, use what is available in your area. The high protein content (24%) in the turkey starter is necessary for keets. Keets raised on turkey starter versus chick starter are markedly larger in size by six months of age than those raised on chick feed. To get them started, sprinkle just a wee bit of feed on a paper towel in the bottom of the brooder. (Do not sprinkle on manure, and remove any feed that gets manure on it.) Following natural instinct, the keets will peck at the feed and begin eating. Always keep feed available. A mason jar with a screw on type chick feed dish will fit nicely in a corner of the brooder. Keets who are not permitted to free feed at this point must be fed 5-6 times daily.

At one week to ten days old it is ok to introduce lettuce, dandelion leaves and grass. By twelve days of age introduce insects, worms, cracked corn, grit, oyster shell and wild birdseed. Use white millet sparingly, **for training purposes only.**

When handling the keets, choose a phrase to use consistently before awarding them with white millet. Sit on the floor and call them to you. If they come, award with a few seeds of white millet. For some reason, I came up with "Guinea guinea want some seeeeeeed? "It may sound funny, but it worked! To this day, I can walk outdoors and see not a guinea in site, call them, "Guinea guinea, want some seeeeeeed?" and they come running from out of nowhere! It sure does come in handy when one needs to go away, and wants to put the guineas in the henhouse earlier than the normal routine. I have come to realize by trial and error, white millet is the ultimate seed that could possibly pass their beaks. Beware, this is pure WHITE millet, not red, yellow, or mixed seed containing millet. Stores that sell birdseed, wild birdseed, birdhouses, feeders, and such will often carry millet. Some feed mills may be willing to special order it. Often garden supply centers carry birdseed. Wild bird centers may sell it by the pound. I have found it to be far less expensive when purchased in the largest size available.

About 6 weeks of age, the keet's starter food can be switched gradually by mixing increasing amounts of turkey grower to the turkey starter, gradually weaning them off the starter feed. Again, some feed mills carry only a combination mix of turkey starter/grower instead of each type separately. Should this be the case, the keets can remain on the starter/grower until they are released from the "nursery".

My keets finish a 50# bag of medicated turkey starter/grower or two before they are released from the "nursery" in the henhouse. The number of bags will vary depending on the number of keets raised at one time. The age at which the keets are released from the "nursery" is dependent on the age they were when moved from the brooder to the nursery plus six weeks additional time in the nursery.

When changing feeds, they need a week or two to wean off of the grower. Mixing small amounts of the new feed with the old, decreasing the amount of grower mix each time is the best way to switch food. By 12 weeks of age, medicated food needs to be completely removed from the diet. This will prevent any medication residues from being deposited in the eggs. Egg production can start as early as 16 weeks old.

Commercially balanced feed mixes might include a combination of the following ingredients in turkey starter/grower, developer, finisher, and layer mixes: corn, oats, wheat, barley, rice, rye, ground buckwheat, bone meal, trace minerals such as iron, iodine and manganese, alfalfa, soybean meal, meat meal, salt, limestone, vitamins, lysine, and others. Feed mills in various parts of the country vary in what they carry, their recommendations, and names for feeds.

Once released to the henhouse the menu will depend on the other types of birds living there as well. Because the guineas on this farm are housed with chickens, the guineas and roosters have to eat what the chickens eat. I raise chickens for eggs, so a non-medicated laying mash is fed freely in a large galvanized drop feeder that hangs from the ceiling. Hanging the feeder at the same height as the back of the birds helps to prevent food waste from hens scratching in it. Housed without chickens, the guineas would be fed a non-medicated turkey breeder mix of 22 - 24% protein or a game bird feed. During the winter months when guineas are not laying, the amount of protein in the mix can be lower.

Feed is always available to my birds inside the henhouse to protect the feed from the weather and to keep from attracting rabbits, mice and other vermin. Fresh water daily, including scrubbing out the pan regularly makes for healthier birds. This routine also is encouragement for guineas on free-range to return in the evenings.

All birds in the henhouse have access to grit and oyster shell free choice. Because birds do not have teeth, grit is necessary for digestion of foods. Oyster shell is provided as a source of calcium carbonate for maintenance and eggshell formation. The birds know when they need it and will help themselves. Each is kept in a rabbit feeder hanging on the inside of the henhouse wall. Special containers for oyster shell and grit are available, but are rather expensive and the rabbit feeder works just as well.

Guineas will consume about 90% of their diet on free range. They are meat eaters. Their diet consists of grasses, weeds, weed seeds, grass seeds and grains, but mostly bugs, moths, grasshoppers, Japanese Beetles, mosquitoes, spiders, aphids, slugs, ticks, and all other obnoxious insects. They supplement their diet by eating a bit of the food provided in the henhouse in the evening just before retiring to roost.

Scratch feed, such as cracked corn, is only 8.5% protein and high in carbohydrates. Both guineas and chickens love the scratch feed. The more scratch they eat, the less room there is for layer rations, so the protein drops dramatically. Also, the carbohydrates will cause the hen to get too fat and this can cause prolapse or other problems. I offer only a handful on occasion during those hot days of summer.

In the summer take care to provide a water source for the guineas on free-range. I have an extra 5-gallon double walled galvanized waterer setting just outside the potting shed. Guineas need a water supply and could dehydrate easily without one.

In the winter during freezing weather, offer warmed water at least twice daily or use a water heater. Cracked corn is offered in the winter on cold evenings for extra carbohydrates for body warmth and energy. Beware, too much can also add fat when the hens are less active, so don't overdo it! One handful per 3-4 hens is plenty.

Grass is needed for the digestive system of guineas. In the winter, when it is snow covered or on days when for some reason the guineas are not permitted to be on free range, some good, leafy alfalfa hay will be good for them. Hanging a flake of hay in a 2-inch wire or plastic netting will keep it clean, dry, off the ground, and give the birds something to pick at. Alfalfa is high in protein, so beware not to overfeed to birds who do not need lots of protein.

Garden waste and some table scraps, occasionally tossed to the chickens, are enjoyed by the guineas as well. Carrots, lettuce, kale, tomatoes, beets, squash, pumpkins, pumpkinseeds, dried bread crumbs, etc. Beware, once guineas get a taste for tomatoes, they will find them in a vegetable garden and take a bite out of each and every one. Guineas love tomatoes! Don't introduce them to a food you don't want them to eat.

GROWING UP - DETERMINING THE SEX

The sex of a newborn keet is so hard to determine that even hatcheries sell them as straight run (mixed male and female). At first the keets make cute little cooing sounds when eating, or quiet peeping, displaying in no way the aggressive alarm they will produce just a few short weeks away. The song of the guinea when eating millet is so beautiful and soothing, it is hard to imagine these little birds will grow up to produce such a loud warning call, ever! Sex is first distinguished by the difference in the cry of the birds.

Beginning at around 7 to 8 weeks of age the keets will have replaced their first feathers and begin the face shedding process, taking on a new look as if someone colored their skin with purple magic marker...soon to turn white with maturity. Also at this age the keets will begin to practice their adult sounds. The female makes a two-syllable sound that the male cannot imitate, commonly referred to as "Buck-Wheat, Buck-Wheat..." repetitiously. The female is no doubt the noisier of the two sexes. The male can only make a one syllable shrieking sound. During his alert call, "Chi-chi-chi-chi-chi..." is repeated very fast and extremely loud when the male spots movement or sees anything strange on the farm. This is the warning call the guinea is famous for that gives him the title of being the farmer's watchdog. The problem is that the females CAN imitate the male with his warning call of "Chi-chi-chi-chi..." In this case, it is easier to determine the sex of the birds in a yet another way.

By 8 weeks of age helmets and wattles begin to appear. As the young guineas mature, by 12 to 15 weeks, the male begins to develop thicker and larger wattles than the female, making it easier to determine the sex by both wattles and sound. The adult guinea cock will have wattles so large they hang outward and down, appearing to cup under. By a year old the guinea cock stands out with his larger wattles, one syllable sound, a slightly larger helmet, and slightly longer legs than those of the guinea hen. One cannot mistake a male from a female by this point.

To get an accurate count of males versus females is not an easy task since they move continuously. Counting them when roosting in the henhouse is the easiest way.

MATURE BIRDS

Larger guineas need plenty of room when confined in the henhouse during the holding period. A small cage is not appropriate for an extended time period, as the guinea needs to be able to move and stretch, jump and roost. Confining large guineas in small places promotes pecking, fighting, and disease. For these reasons, the lack of space to confine larger birds for long periods of time, (three to four square feet per bird), coupled with the fact that it is nearly impossible to train an older guinea to permit touching and handling, I shy away from offers for mature birds.

Continue to handle guineas throughout their lives.

Chapter

5

Spread Those Wings!

IT'S TIME TO LET GO...

This is without a doubt the most exciting yet somewhat fearful moment for the new owner. For unlike chickens, these guineas could just fly away! But, you need not to worry about them flying too far if the previous guidelines have been followed.

Having been in the nursery for a total of six weeks, it is time to release the keets or older guineas, whichever the case may be. Remember the purpose of the nursery was to train the keets to become accustomed to the building where they are to roost for the night, eat, drink, and feel secure, safe, and dry. Also, during confinement in the nursery, the entire flock, both keets and adult birds were able to see and to eventually accept each other as members of the same flock, making this day of release less stressful for all and the pecking order minor. Having accomplished this, it is time to let go.

When releasing the keets for the first time, morning is best. Once the exterior bird door to the henhouse is opened and the other birds rush out, "nicely" shoo any remaining outdoors and close their entrance door. The ideal nursery would have a door too small for the older birds to enter. This door should be opened or completely removed at this time, giving the keets their freedom and full run of the henhouse.

At first the keets will walk around in the henhouse and explore the nesting boxes and roosts. Some will stretch their wings and take their first short flight. Stay with them for a while and watch, pet them a bit, hold a few, and treat them with some millet. When they have calmed down from checking things out, open the exterior door and allow the chickens, roosters, and whichever guineas may have not left to free-range yet, to enter the henhouse. I always feel more comfortable watching the behavior of the leaders, the head rooster and head guinea and their actions before making my exit. At times it is a chicken hen who will take a peck, her way of telling the keets she is boss. *Ha-ha* ...she may as well try now, for as the keets age, she soon will learn that GUINEAS RULE! The open door to the "nursery" provides a safe area should the keets be frightened or chased by an older bird and want to get away, yet at the same time, the choice to come and go as they please. For the most part, any pecking order will be very mild, so I make my exit and check back in a few hours.

Any new addition to the flock will go through a pecking order, whether it is a keet, young guinea, adult guinea, or chicken. Pecking order amongst domestic fowl is normal. However, should a bird draw blood, remove the injured bird at once to a protected area until it is healed completely. Chickens in particular will peck at a bloody wound until the injured victim is dead. If for some reason the pecking order is disastrous, by all means put the keets back into the nursery, close the door, and try again in a few days.

It is normally a few hours or even a few days, however, before a keet will actually go outdoors. At first a few will go to the poultry opening and peek out, then run back. After a few days, one will get brave and go out to the yard for a while before making a beeline and heading back indoors very quickly. Never force a keet to go outdoors. The purpose of learning the safety and security of its home in the henhouse would be confusing should they be forced out of a place they were taught to stay in! Teaching the keets the safety of this home and where you want them to roost at night is the most important part in keeping guinea fowl domesticated.

At times, a chicken or guinea hen in the poultry yard will chase a keet back inside the building, taking on the role of mother. This is perfectly OK. The worst scenario would be to allow the family pet to be present when the keet first goes outdoors. The small keet could very easily be startled by the sight of this unfamiliar animal, fly up and land outside the fenced area, becoming easy prey or a quick unplanned snack for a dog or cat.

For the first night or two after releasing birds from the nursery, it is lights off so that all inside the henhouse get a peaceful night's rest. Although it is not necessary, I otherwise burn a 15 watt bulb (nightlight) at the ceiling near their exterior door. The bit of light it casts is great for the guineas to be able to see their entrance door to the henhouse should they come back too late from free ranging on a night we were unable to get home in time to stick to the normal routine schedule.

STEPPING OUT

Regardless of the setup of the "yard" surrounding the henhouse, the keet will soon learn to fly over the fence, if there is one, and find its way to the greener grass on the other side. At first, it will not go far, keeping close to the rest of its siblings. The keet will at first just look around, later munch on a few blades of grass, maybe find a bug or two. Soon it will be going in and out of the henhouse as if it owns the place. Eventually the rest of the new flock will follow. However, it will be a while yet before they actually free-range. These birds are discovering a whole new world, so allow them to do so at their own pace.

The new soldiers will at first be startled and possibly fly up to a tree or the roof of the henhouse when approached by a family pet. Likewise, small visitors chasing the keets, eager to try to "catch one to play with" will startle them. The keets will soon learn, and switch from being startled to using their alarming call. Soon the other animals on the farm learn that the GUINEAS RULE! The shrill warning call of the guineas is usually enough to intimidate dogs and cats to turn tail and run. Eventually, they will all get along, just as most farm dogs and cats get along. It is normal here to see the family cats squeeze through the fencing and go into the chicken yard in the mornings to try to beat them to a breadcrumb or other table scrap tossed in. At times a guinea might even be seen getting a drink from the dog's water dish as he lies there watching.

It won't be long before the guineas are investigating the entire property, perhaps roaming further then you would like them to! For now, concentrate on making sure you remain the boss; and when night time comes, help them find their way back into the henhouse if they did not manage to do so on their own.

A routine is nice, and guineas will soon learn if you have one. Mine know the routine, and that the door to the henhouse closes at a certain time each evening. With the shorter days in winter, longer in summer, they tend to adjust just fine and return to their henhouse on their own as nightfall approaches. However, there may be times the keets need some help in getting with the routine. When this happens, two long sticks come in extremely handy. Holding one in each arm as extensions, walk the birds to the gate of the fenced yard, or to the opening of their henhouse. This is a lot easier than yelling at them or giving up and forcing them to sleep in a tree.

As a warning, do not walk around swinging these sticks. Harsh movement will frighten the guineas, most likely causing them to fly up to a tree or rooftop where they will spend the night! Equally as frightening is an unfamiliar umbrella, ski mask, or perhaps a new or different hat of some kind.

Do not allow young children to be either excessively noisy or chase the guineas while trying to walk them into their yard or the opening of the henhouse or they will feel they are being attacked and possibly fly up to a rooftop or into a tree. It will be difficult to get them down until they are ready to come down on their own. This evening routine should not be difficult at all. My daughter has been able to put the guineas away for the evening since she was five years old, all by herself, and takes great pride in the fact that she can control them responsibly.

Should problems in gathering the keets arise, or should one need to put them up for the evening earlier than the routine scheduled time, being able to use the "call for millet" becomes extremely handy.

After a few weeks, the guineas will begin to truly free range. Soon about 90% of their diet will consist of grasses and weeds, seeds of grasses and weeds, and of grains; but mostly bugs, moths, grasshoppers, slugs, Japanese beetles, mosquitoes, aphids, ticks, spiders, and other insects. Upon returning to the henhouse in the evening, the guineas will also usually munch on a bit of the food provided indoors before roosting for the night.

HOME ON THE RANGE

When free ranging, it is typical to see the guineas "hang out" in-groups, usually by age group, eventually combined. The oldest male is likely to become the "leader of the gang." The others seem to keep an eye on him and stay within eyesight.

After a while, if observing closely, it will become noticeable that the guineas have a routine path they follow. As an example, mine are released each morning around 8:30. They will fly to the landing board on top the 6' fence surrounding the chicken yard and wait for me to give them a morning treat of white millet. I walk along that tall fence reaching up and place a bit of millet right by the toes of each bird who waits for me to do so. They enjoy the millet, and I am able to see them extremely close up. Of course I first ask "Guinea, guinea want some seed?" White millet is not a necessary part of the diet, and should be used sparingly. It is like candy is to children! However, millet is certainly helpful in training an otherwise wild bird or hyperactive keet to be tame. When I walk away, the ranging routine begins.

The guineas head in the same direction each morning, seemingly picking up food from the ground as they take each step. Appearing to be as soldiers, they soon spread out a bit, however stay within site of each other. If checked at any one particular time of day, it becomes nearly predictable to approximate which area of the property they can be located on.

Our home sits 1/4 mile off the road, and the guineas have never ranged more than half the distance from the house to the road. As a rule, my guineas spend the majority of their time ranging on the three acres of mowed lawn on this fourteen-acre farm. They love the weeds along the fencerows. Only occasionally do they go into the fields. I have encouraged them to begin their morning by heading straight to my seventeen flowerbeds surrounding the house, coaxing them to follow by calling to them and shaking a plastic jar containing millet, a sound they well know. Having sprinkled millet by my rose garden, the Japanese beetles were noticed immediately and soon looked upon as a morning treat. Once the flower destroying bugs and insects were discovered by the guineas, we were all much happier.

Should the guineas try the greener grass on the other side of the fence between property lines, which they will (knowing no boundaries), it will be necessary to break their routine by being there to turn them around and chase them back, day after day and as long as necessary. Ideally, a henhouse sitting about 1/8 mile from the road and fence row(s) would be nice, as it seems the guineas do not range out further than that. However, having this amount of land between property lines is not always the case, so training will become necessary if neighbors who disapprove live nearby.

Guineas can fly, and it is a real site for sore eyes to see the adult guinea fowl in flight. However, it is usually just for short distances, and about 6-10 feet off the ground. Guinea fowl can fly up to a tree, the roof of a barn or even to the housetop. When returning to the ground, gliding for long distances, their long wingspan is simply beautiful and amazing to watch. There is nothing more pleasing to the eye than to call the guineas home (millet call) and to see them first run... then fly to you from across a field as a group, gliding to a land at your feet, looking up at you, awaiting the treat that will be given with such great pleasure before retiring to roost for the evening in the safe henhouse.

PREDATORS

Guinea fowl are extremely good runners, and will use this speed to run from a problem. However, when attacked by a predator, a guinea can and will fly up to a tree or roof for protection. An exception to this is a broody hen who will try to fight back, more than likely, unsuccessfully.

When a predator is spotted near the farm, whether it is on the ground or overhead, every person and every farm animal will know. The guinea fowl will alert all within hearing distance, making such a racket it can cause a dog to howl and people to hold their ears. The female imitates the warning call of the male, and every guinea in the flock will call out in unison. This sound is the unmistakable warning of an intruder. It is advisable to check things out when this type of commotion is heard.

Warnings may indicate a hawk or owl flying overhead in which case the guineas usually call out and then hide under a pine tree or other nearby protection. Chickens will learn the warning call and quickly run into the henhouse. We have not lost any chickens to predators since adding guineas to our flock.

The hawk is one of many predators of guinea fowl and keets. The hawk pictured on the next page was caught while perched in the goat barn by distracting it with a loud whistle while grabbing its legs. It was released outdoors later after having been brought into the house for petting and pictures. The hawk was calm while held, but pushed off instantly and flew to freedom when the pressure was released from its legs. This particular hawk had been possessed for its own best interest. It had been beating itself into the skylights of the barn roof in an effort to try to get outdoors.

A call was made to the game warden to ask about the Ohio revised code, species of Birds of Prey, and the non-game protected status, including hawks and owls. Kevin Behr, State Wildlife Officer with the Ohio Division of Wildlife had this to say about birds of prey: "According to the Ohio Revised Code, Section 1533.07: No person shall catch, kill, injure, pursue or have in his possession either dead or alive, or purchase, expose for sale, transport or ship to a point within or without the state, or receive or deliver for transportation, any bird other than a game bird, or have in his possession any part of the plumage, skin, or body of any bird other than a game bird, or disturb or destroy the eggs, nest, or young of birds.

The owner of domestic animals or fowl may kill hawks or owls causing damage to domestic animals or fowl while such damage is occurring. Once they prey on a flock of domestic animals, they do not quit. If a bird of prey is killed, the carcass needs to be disposed of and no part can be possessed, including the feathers." Officer Behr advises to bury the bird. Using any part as bait or keeping a feather is against the code. To catch, kill, or possess is a first-degree misdemeanor with a possible 6-month jail sentence and $1,000 fine!

Some birds of prey are exceptions and protected federally. These include the eagles, barn owls, and ospreys.

Revised codes are subject to change, and can differ from state to state. Contact your local game warden to learn of the laws in your own state.

While we saved the life of this particular hawk, should he come back and attack our poultry, according to Officer Behr we have every right to shoot it "while in the act."

Warning calls from the guineas may indicate a fox or coyote, in which case the property owner will become aware of these intruders and could take steps to eliminate them. Stray dogs can be a real problem, as once a dog gets a taste for blood, it will return for more. A call to the dog pound is in order. Egg snatching predators like mink, raccoons, opossum, skunk and snakes could also be present.

Guineas on this farm have warned us of poachers, trespassers, invited guests and uninvited salesmen! We know when the UPS man is here before the doorbell rings, when unexpected company arrives, or when a hot-air balloon is approaching. There will be no mistaking the warning call of "the farmer's best watchdog" when it is heard.

MATING

A guinea hen on free range is monogamous. She is won over by a male during a ritual referred to hereafter as "the chase". Two or more guinea cocks will engage in a race to determine who will win her over. The chase will continue often times for hours. This is most entertaining to watch, as the cocks appear to be like the roadrunner, running at a very fast speed single-file, bodies very still, wings held raised up over their backs, heads leaning forward a bit, legs moving a million miles an hour, and all this while on tiptoe! Take time to sit and observe, as this is most entertaining to watch. They will encircle a huge barn or the house in seconds... over and over and over until one catches up to the other, engages in a very brief scuffle, then continues on until finally one wears out and gives up. When an equal number of hens and cocks exist, they will pair up. However, when the number of female outnumber the male, a guinea cock can easily handle a harem of six guinea hens.

EGGS & OUTDOOR NESTS

A guinea hen can begin laying eggs as early as 16 weeks, depending on the time of year she was born. During "season", a good guinea hen will lay an egg a day. Unlike chickens, guineas do not lay in the winter. In southwestern Ohio, a hen will lay during "season" which is from approximately March through mid September.

Occasionally a hen will make her nest inside a nesting box in the henhouse. However, it is her instinct to nest outdoors, so more than likely, she will choose a well-hidden place on the ground. Choice spots may be in tall grasses along a fence row, inside a pile of abandoned tractor parts or a clump of grass in a field, against a building, or even in a flower bed under a nice sized hosta plant!

Once egg production begins, the hen on range will go to her nest when it is time to lay her egg and afterwards continue to range with the rest of the flock the remainder of the day. It is possible that another hen will deposit an egg in the same nest after she leaves. Sharing a nest is not uncommon. Once the nest has an accumulation of 30-40 eggs in it, the hen will go broody. She will remain on the nest until the keets hatch 26-28 days later.

Often times, a predator will find the nest with a clutch of eggs in it before the hen goes broody and eat them, leaving a mess of broken shells for the hen to find the next day.

While a hen is on a nest, the mate will hang around during the day, protecting her in a sense, calling out when someone nears the nest. However, once the hen goes broody and remains on the nest overnight, he will often go home to roost with the rest of the flock and abandon her when she needs him the most. It is during this time that a guinea hen is easy catch for a predator.

While broody, it is natural and quite normal to see the hen leave the nest for water and to eat, for periods up to twenty minutes at a time. She knows not to allow the eggs to chill, and a good hen will return before they do.

If a hen is successful in hatching keets in a field, a whole new set of problems arises. The following can problems occur when keets are born outdoors:

- As the keets hatch and begin to move around, the mother may abandon the nest with or without the keets, leaving abandoned eggs that have not yet hatched.
- The mother will move the keets and abandon the nest to get away from unhatched eggs and any dead keets that might attract predators. Depending on the

outdoor temperature, the keets may chill during the move.

- The mother will leave the nest to eat or drink. Predators can get the keets if dampness or chilling does not.
- Keets are very susceptible to dampness and can die by following the mother through dew covered grass. Wet grass and rain are the keets worst enemy, especially during the first two weeks of life.
- Under perfect weather conditions, with no dampness or predators, keets can die from dehydration from being unable to reach water to drink.
- If a source of water is found, the keets may fall in (even a puddle) and drown.

Locating a nest is not always easy. To be successful in finding a clutch of eggs before the hen goes broody will often save not only her life, but will also result in a safer hatch with healthier keets. Should one decide to remove the eggs for hatching in an incubator, leaving four in the nest may encourage the hen to return to the same spot and continue laying.

Should a hen be discovered broody on a nest, one of two choices must be made. Either let her continue where she is and hope for the best, or move her and the eggs to a safe place.

If you are in a safer area and feel no predators will eat your hen for the 26-28 days it will take her to hatch eggs, by all means allow her to do this on her own. However, should you plan to do this, do not disturb her nest should you find her off of it. Remember, she will not go broody until there is a clutch of around 30-40 eggs in it!

If the choice is to let her remain on a nest outdoors, a section of fencing can be put up as a temporary shield to surround her and the nest for some protection from coyote, fox and other such predators. However, she will need to be able to get out for water and food, so the fencing has to be sized and placed accordingly. Checking her daily without disturbing her to discover the hatch will be necessary.

The second alternative is to move the broody hen and her eggs into a prepared location, such as a safe dog kennel. The dog kennel is nice because it is more private like a guinea hen prefers. The kennel should be filled with loose straw/hay mix, and prepared in advance in an undisturbed, quiet area inside a building.

Make a nest in the rear of the kennel. A water dish should be hung high on the door so that the keets cannot reach it. A second hung dish should be filled with food for the mother hen, again, too high for the keets to access. Use a plant-watering container to fill the water dish through the door later.

Moving the hen and clutch is tricky and needs to be done quickly. Have the dog kennel (or similar sized cage) ready inside an outbuilding, not necessarily the chicken coop. A pair of brave hands will be needed for this move, preferably a strong man. Dressed in thick sleeves and gloves, my husband does this part for me and I am his helper. He sneaks up from behind her while I am in the front and she has her eyes on me. She will put up a fight when on that nest, so be extremely cautious. Her behavior will be ferocious with pecks aimed to do serious bodily harm. The strong person behind should quietly and quickly bend over and grab her over her wings, facing AWAY from him. He should hold her out away from his body as he quickly moves to the kennel already in place. (Do NOT carry her by her legs, as they are tenderer than chicken legs and not to be used in the same manner, as people are known to carry chickens, hanging them upside down.)

Meanwhile, the second person is needed to gather the clutch immediately, placing each egg in regular egg cartons for safer movement, then rushing to be first to reach the kennel. Place the eggs carefully in a similar clutch in a prepared nest in the very back of the kennel. The mother is carefully, but quickly, released inside the kennel, and door closed immediately. Add water to her dish and walk away.

After a few days, the broody hen will come to trust one calm, slow-moving caretaker to provide food and reach in to get the water dish to replace it with fresh, clean water. Once keets arrive, a chick waterer must be provided for the them, along with a mason jar chick feeder.

We have successfully carried a broody hen to a kennel when to our surprise the clutch was in process of hatching! Keets and pipped eggs were actually carried to the prepared nest in the egg carton too - very carefully of course because the lid would not close! On each separate occasion, the hen broody in the field has successfully hatched keets in the kennel provided, then taught them to eat and drink while in the dog kennel.

HATCHED BY A HEN

Once the keets have hatched under a hen, the perfect time to sell extras is as soon as the ordered amount is eating and drinking. Day old keets are best for the new owner to begin with, as well as easing the care you will have to provide for them. Gathering feisty little keets born in a field will not be as easy as those born in a kennel.

The hen in confinement in the kennel will gladly exit when the door is left ajar, and regain her place with the rest of the flock. She may look back once or twice, but her desire to eat bugs and free range will outweigh her desire to continue confinement in a cage with all those keets. Take caution when setting her free. Set the kennel on the floor so the keets do not fall to the ground when trying to follow her. Move the keets to a prepared brooder where the circle of raising tamed, domestic keets for *Gardening With Guineas* can successfully begin again.

Problems
&
Suggestions

NOISE LEVEL

When keets first discover their voices, they use them constantly, complaining about every movement in sight, whether it be the family pet, a squirrel, an airplane overhead, or a leaf blowing in the wind. When one starts the chatter, they all jump in. These are the adolescent times, and like most children, young guineas can be extremely noisy.

Guineas are very sociable birds. Being chatty is their nature. To talk to them or to offer scratch or white millet is only a temporary fix. Until the guineas reach that first birthday, use patience, forbearance and earplugs, my friend.

Eventually as the birds mature, they will learn to know what belongs on the property and what does not. As an example, rather than to give the family dog heck, they might walk right up to him and drink from his water bowl silently. They will stop "talking" to family members, pets, and the more obvious movements on the property.

Unfamiliar sights or movements will always create a fuss. It is the nature of the adult guinea to stand guard. The guinea hen is much noisier than the guinea cock. While she continues to "buck-wheat" for no explanation, although a little less often, he calls out only when there is a justifiable reason. When the warning call of the male begins, the rest of the guineas will mock him and the entire flock will be heard all over the farm with the shrill "CHI-CHi-Chi-chi-chi..."

Feeding millet or scratch to quiet guineas is only a temporary silencer. Millet should NEVER be used for this reason, as it will greatly decrease the effectiveness of using it for desirable behavior. When enclosed to roost overnight, the guineas are quiet after lights out, otherwise, there is really no way to force them to be totally quiet for any great length of time, other than to keep only the guinea cocks. Unlike raising chickens and roosters, whereas in most cases keeping two roosters in a small flock is one too many, there is no problem in keeping a dozen cocks and few or no guinea hens.

GAWKING

Guineas are beautiful birds and they know it! They just love to look at themselves. Guinea fowl will eventually find a place to hang out where they can see their reflections. This could happen at the edge of a pond, or upon seeing their reflection in a puddle of water. Most often the guineas will find a routine place to gawk, perhaps right in your driveway. When the guineas are making a racket near a car, keep in mind it is most likely they have discovered their reflection in the chrome bumper! Perhaps the discovery will be in the reflection in a house window, or the worse case scenario, by sitting on the deck rail talking to themselves in the huge glass pane patio doors at your neighbor's house... you know, the neighbor who does not like birds! Oh no!

What do you do? Don't panic. Try to explain to the nice neighbor just how upset you are that your birds left home when you have ample bugs and weed seeds to keep a hundred more guineas! Ask them to please make note of the time the birds range over there and explain how you will need a few days to break that routine. Look around for a bird feeder, which may have attracted the guineas in the first place. After all, guinea fowl are birds too. Explain that the guineas on range move continuously, rarely staying in one spot for very long at all. Walk the birds home and try to break that routine pit stop by watching the birds for a few days and turning them in another direction when they are headed to the property line. Most important, get an old inexpensive mirror and hang it on the outside of your henhouse at a level the guineas can gawk at themselves in.

DUSTING

Although guineas do not scratch as chickens do, they do enjoy a good dust bath. A bare spot in the yard is most commonly chosen. The guinea will burrow a perfect body sized pit and manage to make every bit of the dirt from the hole disappear into nowhere. By dusting, every bit of the dirt from this pit is gathered into the wings. When the guinea is finished, it will walk away, shaking the dust from its feathers creating a huge dust storm. Watching one's step when walking toward the henhouse is a good practice, until the dusting area is found. It is common to find several holes in the same area, as the guineas seem to enjoy bathing at the same time. Dirt will need to be carried in from another place to refill the holes, as the dirt removed from them will be no where in sight.

What should you do? Encourage dusting in an out-of-the-way area near the henhouse, by loosening the soil for them in a preferred location. Under a tree where the soil tends to remain soft, as under a tree near the henhouse is a perfect spot. Providing a special place for the guineas to frequent, with this soft ground, mirror, and perhaps a water supply near the henhouse from spring through fall, does encourage frequent "checking in" by the guineas.

WINTER TIME

Guineas are not exactly sure about the white stuff that covers the ground in the winter. In fact, the first time a guinea sees snow, it is quite amusing to watch. When their door to the henhouse is opened on a morning after a snowfall, the guineas brake at the door. Some will experiment and try to walk on it... others will be afraid and remain indoors. Some may fly out and up to a tree, refusing to come back down to roost in the henhouse until the snow melts!

In this case, the call for millet should be tried first. However, the fear of snow can be greater than the love for millet. It might be necessary to put straw on the ground outside the henhouse door, or shovel a spot clean for the guinea to land on. Either that, or wait until the snow melts and hope for the best. At times, tossing a Frisbee near the guinea in a tree will encourage it to come down, but could also make it go up higher into the tree. Others will have no problem or fear and will walk around on any bare spots on the ground. It may be a while before some are willing to walk on snow. Experience comes with age. Allowing a guinea the choice to exit the henhouse onto a snow-covered ground is better than to confine them for long periods of time.

Fresh air and exercise is needed even on the coldest days. Even when snow-covered, the guineas are able to range and find seeds and grasses to munch on. Being confined for long periods of time in too small an area encourages pecking and disease. Unless the temperature or wind chill factor is extreme, it is better to let the guineas free range during daylight hours than to confine them for long periods.

COMMON DISEASES & INJURIES

Immediately isolate any suspected diseased or sick guinea or keet. Using a dog kennel outside the henhouse works great for a safe confinement. Take care to provide food and water, heat if needed, and nice bedding for the bird.

A guinea fowl permitted to free range is virtually disease free. A coop for guineas only should stay relatively clean if the guineas are permitted to free range daily, and roost only overnight. However, in a henhouse with chickens, the bedding is not as fresh. Allowing it to remain wet is asking for problems such as lice, mites, worms, and possibly coccidia. The ammonia smell from chickens can become overbearing if not kept clean, causing possible respiratory problems.

Keeping the henhouse and yard clean is the best prevention of sickness or disease. Rotating a yard is best, but if not possible, using a tiller in the chicken yard occasionally keeps it cleaner and fresher. The birds will just love the loose soil to dust in!

By starting a keet out on medicated turkey starter, keeping the brooder, pens, housing, and immediate "chicken yard" (if applicable) clean, and by allowing the guinea fowl to free range during the day, most all problems and diseases can be avoided.

Coccidiosis is a parasitic disease in the tubes of the digestive system. Coccidiosis causes a lack of energy, diarrhea, and death. Young keets are the most susceptible it seems. Coccidiosis can be found in young keets within a few days after hatching. Starting keets out on medicated starter feed and in a clean brooder are the best preventative measures. If a keet does have coccidiosis, separate it immediately from the rest, for it is very contageous. Proper sanitation is necessary in the brooder to keep the next batch of keets from being contaminated. If coccidiosis is suspected, consult a veterinarian immediately for a positive diagnosis and treatment.

Worms are a fairly common parasite found in chickens. Once again, guinea fowl on free range are not as susceptible. Eating food scraps off the ground in a henhouse or poultry yard contaminated by worm eggs or fecal material can infect a guinea as well as any chickens. Signs are droopiness, unthriftiness and anemia. Treating with Piperazine-17 is effective when following the directions on the bottle. Again, consult a vet for proper diagnosis.

Lice are usually not a problem with guineas. Heavy dust baths will usually remove any of these small grayish parasites. Lice feed on skin, blood, and bits of feathers. A severe case can cause death. Louse powders used on poultry are available, and can be used to treat the guineas, house, and roosts as directed on the product. Consult a vet.

Mites are encouraged by dirty litter. Smaller than lice, they live in cracks and the dirt where they deposit their eggs. Mites feed on blood. Bothered birds are anemic and unthrifty. The entire house has to be fumigated, and birds dusted. Consult a vet.

Birds standing around with fluffed feathers have a problem. Consult a vet who is knowledgeable in treating birds for the most accurate diagnosis.

Local feed stores and farm supply markets often sell medications for farm animals and poultry. Take caution to use any over the counter medications as directed.

When on a farm, there can be many, many animals. After a while, one realizes it is not practical to make pets with all of them. When the vet bill outweighs the value of the animal, as in the value of an adult domestic guinea being under $20 versus a higher vet bill, it becomes practical to have someone who is able, to take the guinea out back and put it down. If you are new to country living, this can be hard to take. However, anyone who has been on a farm for any length of time will not only understand this, but also agree. An exception would be to have a vet determine the cause or disease of a particular animal if there is reason to believe there might be something contagious involved that would spread to the other animals and require immediate treatment or quarantine.

Bottom line is the facts, plain and simple. When the value of a pet outweighs the cost of treatment, by all means see a vet. However, when the cost of the treatment outweighs the value of an animal, have someone put it down. Learn to realize the difference in the two. Treating farm animals should not be confused with treating the family dog, cat, or other special animal.

BOUNDARIES

Guineas on free range will cross the boundaries of a small lot. Even with an acre, they will most likely range to a neighboring property or onto the boundary in front of a property, the road.

It seems the guineas are aware of the insects that gather around a hot road in the evening at dusk, so checking out the pavement for easy pickings makes sense. However, these guineas will become road kill to a speedy driver. Even worse, they could cause a serious accident to a driver who might swerve and hit a tree while trying to avoid hitting the guineas.

Some may have several acres, yet live on a narrow lot with a neighbor right on the other side of the fence. Or, the henhouse may be sitting close to a property line. Not everyone lives dead center in the middle of a huge farm lot where guineas won't range across a fence. Keep in mind guineas are basically wild birds, similar to pheasants, who are being domesticated. It will take time on the owner's part to train a guinea to stay within a boundary if one has neighbors who dislike birds. It will be necessary to learn the routine of the guineas and break it.

In this picture, the guinea cock on the left and guinea hen on the right are eating a bit of millet placed on the landing board on top of the 6' high fence that surrounds the chicken yard.

The following letter is an example of the courtesy displayed by one owner of a pair of guinea fowl, copied and distributed to surrounding houses prior to releasing their offspring on her one acre lot in the suburbs:

Dear Neighbors,

So far I have heard mostly positive remarks in regards to my Guinea Fowl. There have been several complaints, and I have done my best to solve these problems. I'm sure you have seen my two adult Guineas roaming the neighborhood and your yard frequently as they search for bugs and ticks. I now have 9 keets (baby Guineas) and they will be released and free to roam starting this weekend. With that many Guineas they will soon be roaming a wider area to get all the bugs they need for their diet. I will do my best to continue to encourage them to spend most of their time near my house. I can not keep them locked up continuously because they are not domesticated chickens. Currently I release my birds at 8AM, and lock them up for the night at around 6PM. This way they are safe from predators and not roosting in your trees, keeping you up at night. If you have any complaints or comments, please feel free to contact me at ###-####. I hope that everyone enjoys the Guineas as much as I do.

Sincerely,
Christina Abramowicz

A handout such as this allows time for feedback from neighbors prior to getting guineas or as in the case above, prior to releasing more that you may already have. In the case of having to deal with a grumpy neighbor, it may be better to weigh out any problems in advance so as to avoid a potential feud later.

There seem to be many people living in agricultural areas who for one reason or another do not want guineas ranging through their yard. Most do not know the facts about guineas nor the benefits that they can reap from them. Some fear a bird of this size, others are unaware that the guineas will not destroy their gardens. Taking the time to explain the many benefits listed in this book is usually enough to turn a grumpy neighbor into a happy one.

Unfortunately, there are also those few who will not accept any explanation for whatever reason. The decision in this case of what to do or how to handle this problem can become a troublesome one. In this case before making a hasty decision NOT to raise guinea fowl, you should be aware of your right to raise guinea fowl.

The rules, regulations and laws in each state vary. If you need to contact some officials, the following two are a good place to start:

First call the Zoning Board in your own area to be certain it is permissible to raise guinea fowl on your own property based on zoning and land usage rules.

Also call the office of your State Vet through the State Department of Agriculture, Animal Industry, for access to specific laws, the right to raise, and regulations regarding raising guinea fowl in the state in which you live.

ANECDOTES

- A guinea cock confined constantly will run a rooster ragged. However, guineas and roosters will get along just fine when the guinea is on free range and roosts in the henhouse overnight or when confined in a henhouse for a few days during extreme weather conditions.

- The best possible solution to prevent a pecking problem is to allow ample floor space per bird. Pecking often begins with the toes. Chickens especially, will then savagely attack bloody birds until death occurs. Use a cage to separate any bloody or severely pecked bird until completely healed. Keeping the cage inside the henhouse where all birds can see each other as the injured bird heals, helps to eliminate a pecking order when the harmed bird is re-introduced to the flock after it has fully recovered.

• Limping is a common injury with guineas. Their legs are not as strong as those of a chicken. Most limping guineas will hang around in the chicken yard until their leg heals within a week or two, and then rejoin the flock on range. Do not carry guineas around by the legs. Provide plenty of room for landing in an area where they are expected to jump up or down from. A wet or slippery brooder floor can contribute to leg problems or foot wounds in keets.

• Crooked toes can be a sign of injury, of poor genetics or too much in-breeding, or can also happen during incubation caused by low humidity. Some crooked toes may straighten out on their own in a few days. Some owners tape the toes using thin cardboard as a foot pad and a cloth-like first aid tape to hold it in place in an effort to help straighten the toes. Some crooked toes will not straighten. Curled or crooked toes could be a sign of a more severe deformity that will show up later. Feeding a pre-mixed medicated turkey starter to keets with the necessary vitamins and minerals, including B2, helps prevent many problems.

• Bring new, unrelated bloodlines into the flock now and then help minimize any inbreeding problems.

• Molting is the process of replacing feathers. Molting can be brought on by seasonal changes, unfavorable housing conditions such as a house that is too dark, or by stress. Like chickens, guineas do not lay eggs during a molt. They need to utilize all the protein in their diet to grow their new feathers.

- Save guinea feathers for crafts and flower arrangements. Craft and specialty shops will often purchase feathers, especially the spotted feathers of the pearl guinea!

- Although it is true guineas like most types of seeds, there is no need to be concerned when planting a garden. Guinea fowl do not scratch, as chickens do. Guineas will not bother seeds that are planted beneath the soil.

- Guineas will eat both tomatoes and bees. Take precautions to raise either in a protected area. Feeding garden scraps to guineas is encouragement for them to find and eat the same plant growing in a garden. Don't toss them pumpkin to eat and then expect them to stay out of the pumpkin patch!

- A quick headcount inside the henhouse each evening is the best way to keep track of your birds. A stray may wander in a bit late, wanting to be with the flock after you have closed the door for the evening. Keep on the lookout. Should a stray get home too late, it is to your benefit to make a second trip out to the henhouse to let it in. Otherwise, it will awaken before the roosters, and set off an alarm for all to hear at the crack of daybreak, if not before! A guinea out at night is also easy prey for a predator.

- When a guinea trained to roost in the henhouse suddenly does not come home one night, it is safe to assume one of two things. Either she went broody on a nest, or was snatched by a predator. Often a guinea cock will be behave strangely and be unwilling to go into the henhouse. More than likely, his mate is on a nest and he may want to stay nearby. When this happens, it is easy to find the hen by keeping an eye on him.

He will point you in the right direction. Try to locate her before a predator does.

- Check with a game warden to be certain of your rights before shooting predators. If it is legal, shoot to kill. Traps could possibly go off on free ranging guinea fowl instead of the predator. Once a predator gets a free meal, it will return for more.

- Spending a night in a tree, possibly because the evening routine was not the norm, due to the fear of a snow-covered ground, or maybe because a daytime predator frightened the bird, or for whatever other reasons, on occasion, will happen. Cross your fingers and hope for the best. The guinea will get thirsty and hungry and come down eventually if you are unable to coax it down with white millet. Using a Frisbee tossed above the guinea may encourage the bird to come down, or might frighten it to go even higher into the tree.

- If one begins with adult guineas who roost in trees, keets will eventually follow in their footsteps. It is best to retrain the adults to roost in the henhouse before any new keets arrive.

- For years I have been anticipating a hatch to include a chicken-guinea cross with no such luck. I have seen a rooster breed guinea hens on several different occasions. The off-spring, known as a guin-hen, is said to resemble a turkey with a body the size of the chicken and a bare head and neck like the guineas. Any offspring are said to be sterile.

- Keeping the water trays full in the incubator is very important. At hatch time, the use of a wet bulb to check humidity level can be reassuring. If using a wet bulb, a dirty wick can cause incorrect readings. If the water trays have been kept properly filled, any unhatched keets are most likely deformed or weak. Let Mother Nature take her course, and do not help a stuck keet. Only the fittest should survive to procreate.

- When raising different aged keets who still require brooding, it is important to keep in mind the temperatures necessary in the brooder for the youngest, and to hang the heat lamp accordingly so that the older keets can get away from the heat source if they desire. A wall in the middle of the brooder comes in handy when the age difference is too great. Pecking order is common even with very young keets. Most brooder-aged keets will mix nicely, however a sharp eye is necessary at the first sign of trouble. Often a runt will be picked on tremendously. Allow at least 6 square inches of floor space per keet in the brooder.

- When beginning with a brand new henhouse, guineas, and no other birds, the guineas or keets can have the run of the entire henhouse rather than be confined inside a nursery for the 6-week period. A 6-week confinement inside the henhouse is still necessary. Guineas should not be permitted to go outdoors to an attached enclosed yard during this training period. Avoid the temptation.

- Monitoring eggs for development is possible beginning on day 10 of incubation. When looking closely through the egg while holding it closely against an egg candler or a mag light in a dark closet, you should be able to see tiny blood vessels looking spread like a spider running through the interior of the egg. Infertile eggs will be clear and can be discarded. Toward the end of incubation light will shine only through the air cell end while the rest of the egg appears to be very dark.

7 *Guinea Fowl Online*

THE INTERNET

Keeping track of dates to start seeds and their germination dates for the greenhouse was becoming a lot of work, constantly changing. Always rewriting to squeeze in a new variety, my paperwork and notes were a mess. "Ahhhhhhh, a computer," I thought to myself. Finally an excuse to get one! In December 1996 my computer arrived. After the initial shock upon seeing all those boxes and wires, I pulled out the instruction map and put it together. A booklet told me how to properly turn it on and shut it down. I was off!

Excel, a wonderful program that came preinstalled, was my first challenge to learn. Playing with the charts, I managed to create a list for seed propagation that can be easily updated, new seeds inserted, sorted at the click of a button, and is absolutely wonderful.

Well, it was only January 1997 when I discovered in a local software shop a sign that said "Limited Internet Access, $5.00". I wondered…"*What is the Internet?*" Having no clue what I was getting into, I paid the man $5.00 and went home to my computer to find out.

That was the beginning. Two months later, I found a local ISP with a decent price for unlimited access and began to "surf" the web. My first stop was in a gardening chat room to meet a twelve-year pen pal online. Upon entering the room, a name or handle was requested. She suggested we choose flower names for our handles. She chose California Poppy, her state flower. Fritillaria Meleagris is the botanical name for the Guinea Hen

Flower, a spring perennial bulb. I chose Fritillaria as my handle, and later shortened it to Frit. It is quite appropriate since I raise both Guinea Fowl (of the species Numinda Meleagris) and flowers, including the Fritillaria Meleagris.

Via surfing, I discovered very little information on raising guinea fowl. When coming across a site about chickens in Geocities, I clicked to "get my own free homepage". It was natural for me to decide to put up a site about raising guinea fowl for the small farm or homestead flock. This was the beginning of my website, entitled:

Frit's Farm   ~Gardening With Guineas~

The e-mail started coming in with both compliments about the site and questions regarding raising guinea fowl. In April 1998 the addition of a message board for questions and answers regarding raising guinea fowl was added. My thoughts were to eliminate much of the e-mail by posting answers others might find helpful on an interactive message board online. The website has gained popularity, having several regular visitors as well new visitors daily. Many post comments to questions or ask some that require fairly long responses. Visitors come from all over the world, including Africa, where guinea fowl still roam wild in the countryside.

The website is not flawless. Because the site is graphic intensive, it is slow to open with a connection less than 56K. Patience while opening please.

http://www.guineafowl.com

If interested in viewing the website, simply enter above URL in the location in the location bar in a web browser. The website contains many photographs, including a hatch in progress, keets and guineas of various ages and colors, a slide show, and pictures of the henhouse both inside and out. The site also includes a link to a guinea fowl chatroom called FOWLHOUSE. Of course it includes photographs of Frit's Farm, the yard, barn, greenhouse and gardens.

Most helpful on the website is a breeder's list. Listed by city and state, these private owners of Guinea Fowl may be willing to sell or take orders for either keets or eggs to help someone get started who may want less than 25-30 keets. These are not hatcheries, but individual homesteads or small farms. In order to purchase less than 25-30 as required by most large hatcheries, it is necessary to pick keets up at the farm, so choose one close to you.

For those who do not own a computer, it is possible to view Frit's Farm by visiting a local library. Most public libraries have two or more computers hooked up to the Internet for free use by cardholders. Librarians are usually more than happy to assist.

The following Q & A section consists of questions and comments taken directly off of the message board at Frit's Farm online. Visitors are encouraged to voice their own opinions by responding to the questions or comments as well.

GUINEA FOWL
COMMENTS, QUESTIONS & RESPONSES

!!!!!! N O I S E !!!!!!

I have 12 - 7 month old Guineas that stay mostly in a one acre enclosure with chickens. The poultry yard is also a small orchard and the location of my compost bins. Needless to say I spend some time there. When I first arrive I receive a "buck wheat" serenade for up to an hour then they usually calm down and go back about their business. I sincerely believe they attempt to communicate with me! I am not overly fond of the "buck wheat" but I tolerate it for the Guineas many other attributes. However I must say I never tire of listening to them when they sound their unique alarm in perfect unison! Also, I find their chirping when feeding delightful and melodious. Enjoy the sounds of this delightful and "one off" (unique) bird !!!

John

_____

GUANO

Frit, I agree with you. We have had up to 50 or so guineas and never found noticeable deposits on our sidewalks (no blacktop here). But the part of the pasture where the Chinese geese stay is a minefield! And Canadian geese leave poops of gigantic proportions. We have raised many keets and a few goslings in the house, until they were old enough to stay outside. The goslings were unbearable. Their litter had to be changed daily - and this from only 2 or 3 goslings at a time. We've always had groups of 6 to 20 keets together at a time, and only their health was a concern for changing the litter - they really do not make much of a mess.

Maureen

_____

SPLAYED LEGS

I tried something to help the 2 keets w/ splayed legs I had and it worked. I took a rubber band (3-1/2" long X 1/8 wide) and knotted it in the middle. I slipped the loops over each leg. I made sure the knots were tight enough to pull the feet under the bird. I watch and adjusted very often (2-3 times a day) till the keet could walk. I called it my guinea truss. I saved one of the keets. I think

I could have saved both if I had been more careful. I sure appreciate this forum. Thanks Frit! I really used all the good info. Thanks---

Guineaman

LIFE EXPECTANCY

A friend asked me a question today, which I am hoping you can answer because I am clueless. What is the average life expectancy of a guinea? Guess you would have to assume no unfortunate run-ins with foxes or raccoons or other critters, which is what we are all working toward. :-)

Thank you, Mary Ann

Re: Life Expectancy

The only way to know this is to keep records and place leg bands on each guinea. I have found that most plastic bands will not stay on, or fall off after a year or so. Some have reported success by using metal leg bands. I have never seen documentation on the life expectancy of a Guinea Fowl. "BOSS" is the leader of my flock and stands out among the rest. Boss is around 9 years old.

Frit

ADDING NEW KEETS

Our four keets we have are doing great! They are so cute. They are eating and sleeping machines and are growing rapidly. They are now 1 week old. We have been offered some new keets, which are currently hatching. Would it cause problems if we mix the two batches? Will the older ones harm the younger?

Thanks, Mary

Re: Adding New Keets

At this young age there should be no problem at all by raising keets a week apart in age together. I would be certain the new keets are eating and drinking well, and moving around well before putting them in with the older ones. At first, the older keets may even be afraid of the newbies! But this doesn't last, and soon they will all mingle and get along just fine. The heat in the brooder will need to be set to the required temperature for the youngest in the group. If the brooder is large enough, any keet who is too warm can just move away from the heat source with no problem.

Frit

GUINEA MATING

We were given one guinea; told it was a male. After it fell into the chicken pen 'scared by a bear', I discovered strange eggs, which turned out to be 'his'. Was looking for a female; now am looking for a male. Have several local leads, but all are waiting for keets to hatch. My main question is: I was told that guineas mate for life. I have found no information either to deny or confirm this concept. Do you know? This was a full-grown guinea, so I wonder if she will accept a different male, and if, when mature, age matters. This is all new to me - chicken and guinea - and I love it. I'm so happy to have found your web site.

You've done a great job, and I've learned a great deal just in one evening of reading mail and answers. Thank you.

Tricia A

Re: Guinea Mating

Not to worry, your hen will find a new partner and remain faithful to him as long as he is around. If you have several guinea cocks, one will win her over during "the chase". However, he will take on a harem if necessary, depending on the number of cocks to hens in your flock.

Frit

_____

MIXING CHICKS & KEETS

I have nineteen chickens on my property. They are in a large coop, at night. During the day, they free-range over ten acres. I would love to raise four to six guineas, because of the tick problem here in Connecticut. I have two concerns. One is noise, and that is definitely not okay. Also, I know how to raise chicks in a brooder, and assume it's basically the same with keets, but then what? Do I simply place the young guineas in the coop with the chickens one night? When does it become okay to let them eat the chicken feed? And, do I need to confine them in the coop for a week or so, like the chickens so that they know where to return every night? I'd really like to give it a try, but I want them to have a fair shot at making it, you know? If you can help, I would appreciate it. My kids would get a kick out of the guineas.

Thanks, Beau

Re: Mixing Chicks & Keets

Brooder temperatures for keets are basically the same. Whereas a keet starts out in a brooder 95 degrees, a chick can start at 90. Medicated turkey starter is higher in protein than medicated chick starter, so keets will get off to a better start with the turkey starter. However, they will survive if raised on medicated chick starter. However, keets raised on medicated turkey starter will grow faster and stronger. Chicks are a lot bigger and grow faster at first than the keets, who will soon pass them in size. I have successfully raised chicks and keets in the same incubator (by starting chicken eggs seven days later), and brooder (by adjusting the heat for the keets, and by raising the keets on medicated chick starter.

When it is necessary to confine keets and chicks or guineas and chickens together, it is necessary to feed chicken food rather than turkey food. This is unfortunate for the guineas, but won't harm them. Chickens do not need the excessive protein in turkey food. They will eat it, but excess protein in a chicken's diet is converted to uric acid, deposited as crystals in joints, and can cause gout. Excess protein can also cause reproduction problems when hatching eggs.

As for the noise problem, I would suggest you keep only the guinea cocks. You could butcher the hens.

Keets will need to be confined in the henhouse longer than chicks. My advice is six weeks. I suggest allowing your children to handle and play with the keets beginning on day two. Lucky keets who are handled often will be extremely tame and playful with children, often following them around like puppies, wanting to be held, petted, and carried around on a shoulder!

Frit

TAKE FRIT'S ADVICE

When my guineas were first allowed to free range, they returned to their coop at night. Then one night they decided to roost in the tree behind the pole barn. I foolishly allowed them to stay. This tree does not have very dense foliage and that night I lost two to owls. I learned a sad lesson, bought some millet to entice them back to the coop, and have decided to try not to break any more of your rules! ON a happier note, the guineas finally found the vegetable garden and are doing a good job on the insects. Now if they could just learn to weed!

Linda

MOVING GUINEA NESTS

In my chicken coop, I have a nursery area approximately 4' X 11' X 6' high. If I put a broody guinea hen and her eggs in this nursery, will she stay on them or just fly up to a roost? Also, I have heard that if you handle the guinea hens eggs, she will not go back to them. Is this so?

Kate

Re: Moving guinea nests

The nursery is not very private. A guinea hen likes to make her nest in a secluded place. I have found the dog kennel, basically having three solid walls, a solid top and bottom with wire door on front and small "windows" at the top of each side to be perfect for her. When the eggs are placed in there first, she really doesn't have a large area to think about moving around in, and has always continued the hatch. Putting the kennel in a quiet area inside a barn or shed where children or visitors will not bother her is extra encouragement.

Frit

CORRECT TEMPERATURE

I have been getting mixed information on the incubation temperature for guinea eggs. Some say 100 degrees, some say 98 degrees. I am using a HOVA-BATTOR #1602N, with a Automatic Egg Turner. Can you advise what is best on temperature control during hatching?

Charlie

Re: Correct Temperature

The temperature in most cases is the same for chicken and guinea eggs. My incubator came preset at 99 1/2 degrees, standard for most bird eggs. A knob on top can adjust the heat as needed. It is important to read the directions that come with each individual incubator, and follow them closely! There are so many different kinds, some have self-turners, some don't have fans, others do not have water grooves. Make sure you follow the instructions from the manufacturer. The temperature should be maintained throughout the entire hatch.

Frit

ON THE LIGHTER SIDE

Just wanted to let you know that I am becoming known as the "lady with the guineas" in my area. We have a lot of visitors to our farm since we raise fish for the wholesale fish market and are the only aquaculture farm in this part of the state. Used to be that everyone wanted to see the ponds. Now it's the guineas! This is chicken farming country and guineas are a novelty. Seems that everyone's grandparents raised guineas and they bring back good memories. All have a guinea tale to tell. I've had lots of requests for keets when and if mine breed. Of course I refer everyone to your great website since I had no idea what I was doing with these birds until I found you.

Linda

AGAINST ALL ODDS

I posted a question about three weeks ago about cooling eggs. Two hens were on the same nest. After a few more days, one quit setting. The other stayed. She was under a pile of barbed wire about 8' X 8' across and about 3' high, w/fence posts that were grown thick with weeds and grass. I couldn't get to them.

I've never, EVER had a guinea hen set in the wild that didn't get killed before the hatch. Well, she did it, a 100% hatch! Looks to be about 23-30 babies.

During the hatch, she would get off the nest and carry the empty egg shells about ten yards away and dump them. Then she would hurry back to the nest. Is this normal?

Tony O.

Re: Against all odds

Evidently her spot in the barbed wire was extremely safe from predators. Unfortunately, most guinea hens will leave the nest as soon as many fidgety keets are moving around, often times to a less safe place, and through wet grass. The smell of the remains in the hatched shells as well as those eggs that did not hatch encourage predators, including snakes. Evidently she knew this, and carried them off so as to keep her ideal nest! I give her credit for being a smarter mom than most guinea hens!

Frit

GAMEBIRD FOOD

I am getting near the bottom of my bag of medicated turkey starter/grower, so I went to the feed store. There I found several varieties of gamebird foods. They had starter, grower, and some sort of breeding food. I crossed my fingers and picked out grower. Hope that will be okay. What do you think? Will it be a problem? The keets are now between 4-5 weeks.

Thanks again, Mary Ann

Re: Gamebird Food

Feed mills in various parts of the country offer different pre-mixed foods. How your birds are housed, separated by age groups, and whether they are in a brooder or not will determine the food choice. After you raise the first flock through adulthood, the next group to be released from the "nursery" will most likely need to be fed differently because they are moving in with older guineas or chickens. Until keets leave the brooder, if possible keep them on medicated turkey starter. Always buy it in 50 pound bags for cost savings. If no other birds exist, the food of choice after leaving the "nursery" would be the grower. Later you might switch to a developer then mash or laying ration (breeder food) specially formulated for the production of eggs. If raising guinea fowl only, some feed mills offer a maintenance ration to be fed when the birds stop production for the winter. Most feed mills will give good advice as to which food to use at various stages, or have pamphlets listing each food available, the stages, and offer suggestions.

Frit

GUINEAS AND CATS

Hi. I'm considering getting some guineas cause I've heard so many good things about them. I have an organic market garden and thought they sounded just right for some additional pest control. One of my concerns, however, is with another of my pest control strategies - cats. We have several to help with the rabbit, mouse, vole, and etc. populations. Are the two (cats and guineas) compatible, and if so, how long would I have to keep the keets protected from the cats? Thanks.

Tim

Re: Guineas and cats

Keets are usually in a brooder and then moved on to the nursery until they are at 7-12 weeks old (depending on when they were born and heat requirements) before being released to range outdoors. By that time, they are big enough to fly up to get away from cats. My cats have never caught a keet or guinea, and one even accidentally spent the night in the henhouse with all of my birds! (was it ever frightened by morning... and the first one out!!!) My cats go right in the chicken yard, to try to beat them to a breadcrumb... no problem. We must have a dozen barn cats here. "GUINEAS RULE" you know!

Frit

LAVENDER GUINEA FOWL

Hi, I am a regular visitor on this page and I like it very much because I've learned a lot in regarding to raising guinea fowl because I am a beginner to this business. Last year we started a bird farm and most of them are common guinea fowls. Now we have more than a hundred breeders. My question is, in the beginning we have had pure pearl guineas but now every hatch we have, there are some lavenders. What is the reason why, We have no lavender breeder at all. I hope somebody can answer my question.

Best Regards, Nestor

Re: Lavender Guinea Fowl

I have had lavender hatch from royal purple. I have had buff, and a slate hatch from pearl. It is in the genes. Somewhere in the background of your pearls, was a parent who was not pearl. I think when one orders a certain color, that is what they get, selected from a group of keets. However, those are not guaranteed PUREBRED with a pedigree, which would explain how keets could be any of 17+ colors, based on background genes.

A hatchery can sell a certain species, and not list the species as purebred. When ordering a particular color keet, you will get what you order! However, the progeny may be potluck somewhere down the line.

Frit

WON'T GO IN THE OUTHOUSE[1]

A curious situation: Day before yesterday... filled their water bowl, feed bowl, sprinkled some millet in the outhouse. Usually they wait for me to walk away, and then head in for food. So, I presumed they did. (They're still roosting in the trees, so I leave the door to the outhouse propped open. Admittedly, I haven't been trying hard enough to get them into the outhouse at night. I noticed recently the roof was leaking... so until I get that patched up, I'm not going to force them there... They're literally a few feet from my bedroom window at night... so although it's not ideal, it might be better than the outhouse for the time being.) ANYWAY (enough excuses)...

When I went to bring them food and water the next morning... I noticed that all the millet was still there. And their food & water didn't look touched. That was odd. But odder still, among their droppings were a few very red looking droppings or smears of some sort. I'd have suspected some sort of berries because that's sort of what it looked like, but it's not that time of year; besides, why would there be smashed berries in the outhouse?

Anyway, I went back today. And again, same thing--millet still there (which is very, very weird, as they usually don't leave

---

[1] A guinea home converted from an old outhouse no longer in use.

one grain behind) and the food and water looked untouched. And the red droppings looked like they'd gotten a bit darker and browned. Blood? Everybody looks healthy. They hang out by the outhouse. But it doesn't seem that they're going in. What could this mean?

Lexi

Re: Won't Go In The Outhouse

I have problems with chickens & possums & raccoons; the varmints (once they have found they can get dinner (meat and eggs) in the coop, they will come back frequently (the raccoons tend to alternate days) to dine around dusk. If the critter gets several of the flock the remainder seems to get the idea the coop is not a good place to be and they will try to roost elsewhere. I had to check the coop for varmints and then chase them in to re-train them; it took less than a week. I haven't had much experience with guineas yet, but suspect they are more nervous and will take longer to retrain. I would have expected you to have found loose feathers from the struggle and noticed fewer birds in the flock if a predator was active. I do not know if a snake stealing eggs would frighten the birds at all.

daveb

Re: Re: Won't Go In The Outhouse

My hen was back on her nest soon after a snake stole several of her eggs.... Big black snake too, even the bluejays were ticked off at him! (The yelling bluejays actually pointed out the snake to me)

Christina

───────────

Re: Re: Re: Won't Go In The Outhouse

A fenced yard attached to the henhouse provides protection for guineas who stay behind when recovering from a foot problem or other injury. A fenced yard also keeps predators out of the henhouse. The yard serves as an entrance to the henhouse the guineas will be free to use at any time throughout the day, as the henhouse door can safely be kept open for them to access food and water as needed. The guineas will fly over the fence. Be sure to have a landing board on the top edge of the fence for them!

Frit

INCUBATORS

I am going to try hatching some guinea eggs this spring. Can I mix them with peafowl eggs? Can I start eggs at different times?

Thanks, Fran

RE: Incubators

For the best results, eggs should be of the same size and type. However, I have successfully added chicken eggs to an incubator with guinea eggs on day 7 of the hatch. Chickens hatch in 21 days, whereas keets hatch in 26-28 days.The idea is to have them hatch at the same time. The conditions on the inside of the incubator during the hatch will be somewhat different. Having removed the vent plugs there will be more air movement, also higher moisture from the wet, hatching keets. To start cooler eggs than those in the incubator on random dates is asking for a smaller hatch rate. It would be best to have a second incubator if it is used very often for different egg types and needed at the same time.

Frit

ODD EGG IN THE INCUBATOR

My daughter found a very tiny bird egg below a pine tree after a storm. I had no clue what the blue egg was from. It was about the size of a thumbnail. It was so small, I allowed her to put it in the incubator with guinea eggs, thinking nothing would come of it. One day when I went to turn the eggs, that tiny bird had hatched! I was shocked! It was not much bigger than a carpenter ant and had a huge head! Well, we mashed some of the turkey starter with warm water and fed it with a medicine dropper every time we possibly could nearly around the clock, one drop at a time. It lived for four days, and had grown during that time! It was sad that the little bird did not survive, however it did survive longer than we ever imagined it would, and it taught us a lesson not to fool with Mother Nature.

Frit

STRANGE GUINEAS

These guineas do not like millet. I don't care how much I throw out - they ignore it. The strategy now is to throw a handful of cracked corn to the chickens and then throw like CRAZY into the neas-neas pen. Once I've got one or two, I've got the rest. This is based on three nights. Will they go up better when it gets colder? Happiness from Capria Mountain, Dawne.

Re: Strange Guineas

The millet used for training needs to be pure white millet. Red millet, yellow millet, or a wild birdseed having millet as part of the mix is just not the same thing. Guineas do like cracked corn and other foods as well, however, pure white millet cannot be beat for training.

Training the guineas to roost indoors at night should not be a problem if they were confined in the henhouse for six weeks to begin with. Most will be eager to go in to roost for the evening, after munching on a bit of chicken food and getting a big drink of clean, fresh water! Of course, an exception will be helping the new young guineas find their way in for the first day or so.

Frit

GUINEA QUESTIONS

Thank you! I'm so happy to have found you!!! I'm not only a newbie at chickens and guineas, but with the net as well. The only time I get to do much with it is during my lunch hour, or breaks, because I don't have a computer, (only at work.)

My guineas are young, fully feathered, and about 6-8" tall. I don't know when they were born. Since I got them, they have been on chick starter. I didn't know I was supposed to give them turkey starter. Should I switch? Also, they are in a coop divided in half, (I have 4 bantys with 13 teeny chicks on the other side) with a 1' X 2' door to the outside, which has an 8' X 8' fenced in area. I know for them to realize this is their home I must keep them there for at least a month.

I have two adult males that free range, but since I got the babies, they won't leave the fenced in area. They pace constantly, around the fence. At night though, they go to their trees. Is it safe to let them in? I want to train ALL of them to sleep in the coop at night. If I can let them in, will they change their ways? The adults get cracked corn for a treat. Is this good for them? What other "treats" cam I give them to enhance my wishes---bride them.

For the little ones, I cut up the greens from the garden such as lettuce, carrot tops, onion tops, turnip greens, and kale. I have slipped in a few slices of bread and an apple cut up too. Should I continue this, or save this stuff for my bribes?

These young ones (old ones too) are NOT friendly and very skittish when I enter the coop. Most often, they escape through the little door to the fenced in area. If I shut the door, will they get friendlier with me? They really go nuts when anyone enters the coop. The chickens don't give a rip. In fact, they know if I'm on my way that means goodies or fresh water. Please advise ASAP so I can act ASAP. Thank you so much for your time and any help you offer.

Cec

Re: Guinea Questions

It is important that your keets be on a medicated food at this time. If the chicks have access to it, then the medicated chick starter is called for. However, if they are alone, medicated turkey starter is even better due to the higher protein content.

The keets need to be able to get under a heat lamp or brooder until they are fully feathered, at about six weeks. Also, they need to be confined inside the building for a full six weeks before they are permitted to go out to the chicken yard. A caged "nursery" area is best, so that they and the adult birds may see each other without safety problems.

I would advise penning the adults for a six-week period of retraining so they will roost in the henhouse, else the keets would eventually follow in their footsteps and roost in trees.

White millet is the best "treat" for training purposes only, and to be used extremely sparingly. Garden scraps are good, however giving guineas a taste for a delicious garden now is encouragement to help themselves to those growing in the garden when on free range later. To your list of garden scraps can be added pumpkin, tomatoes and strawberries, but beware, they will find these things in the garden later! Don't encourage them to eat something you might later regret!

Keets purchased as day old and handled many times daily will not fear people. They will want to be held, come when called, and will look forward to being held and petted.

Frit

EATING THE EGGS

When the guineas start laying eggs, how do I know which eggs are fertilized and which ones aren't? Can you eat fertilized guinea (or chicken) eggs or should you remove all the males from the pen so the hens lay unfertilized eggs? Do Guinea eggs taste like chicken eggs? If a hen lays ten eggs and then begins to sit on them, at what point do they go from edible egg to embryo? Will a hen sit on unfertilized eggs?

Abby

Re: Eating The Eggs

Both chicken hens and guinea hens will lay eggs if there is no rooster or cock. If one has a rooster for the chicken hens, and a guinea cock for the guinea hens, the chances are a large percentage of the eggs laid will be fertile. Eggs for food should be collected daily and refrigerated. (Chicken eggs need to be collected several times daily during winter months when they might freeze) Whether the egg is fertile or not does not affect the taste of the egg. Guinea eggs are higher in protein than chicken eggs and rich in flavor. A guinea hen can no more tell if her eggs are fertile than we can. If her eggs are not collected and the clutch accumulates around thirty eggs, she will more than likely go broody on them. Most will be fertile, some will not.

Frit

FEATHERS

I have eight keets that a woman wants to buy. She has a cage, but no light in it. The keets will be three weeks old this Sunday. Should I keep them for her a little longer or are they feathered enough to be without a light?

Bonnie

Re: Feathers

Ideally, people should purchase day old keets. Keets need a 95 degree brooder the first week, and for the temperature to lower by 5 degrees weekly until the keet is fully feathered at about six weeks old. An inexpensive metal lamp shade available from any hardware store that when placed over a 60 watt bulb, provides sufficient heat for a small number of keets, if hung low enough. The sides of the brooder should be solid rather than a cage, so as to avoid drafts and to hold the heat better. A cardboard box works well for the first week or two for a few keets.

Frit

DOORS AT NIGHT

Am I correct in that when you close your birds in for the night you close their walk-in-holes, too? I have been doing this, and then trying to keep a schedule for opening them in the AM and closing them in the PM. Since it gets dark at 4PM in midwinter, I'm assuming I shall have to adjust down in time for 'putting them to bed' as they all seem to want to get inside well before it gets dark. Do you leave a light on for them so they don't have so many 'dark' hours? Or do they just sleep longer?

Thanks for your help, Tricia

Re: Doors At Night

Absolutely correct, Tricia. As for the light, it is not necessary at all. Guinea hens do not lay eggs during the winter months, therefore do not need the extra light to make up a total of fourteen hours of daylight necessary for egg production like chickens require. However, for my own benefit, I do have a 15-watt bulb that burns inside my shed. This casts light on the bird entrance, just in case I am not home on time to put them in for the night. It encourages any stragglers to return on their own, as well as provides some light for me to find my way in there to close their door when I do return late.

Frit

FUNNY-LOOKING CHANGE!

Okay, this may sound dumb…but I went up to feed tonight and noticed a funny looking change in the keets. The feathers seem to have fallen out on their necks, and the skin looks like a child colored it with a purple magic marker. I mean it is bright purple! Is this normal? The farmer we bought them from said they were lavender guineas.

KD

Re: Funny-Looking Change!

Regardless the color of the guinea, they all go through this most funny-looking change. They all will have the look of the purple magic marker. Your keets are growing up!

ON THE OTHER SIDE

Have you ever wondered what might have *really* happened to that missing guinea? Perhaps she was snatched by a predator, is out sitting on a nest in a secluded place, or maybe she just got upset and "flew away from home!" Read the following message I received by e-mail:

> Hi! Last Saturday, I returned from the grocery store to find this huge bird at our bird feeder station. We discovered what it was last night on the net. NOISY! This bird spends time on our very well covered hill and the roofs of our home and the neighbors' houses -- mostly ours because it is flat. It is friendly. In fact,

when I was making a call Saturday to try to discover what it was it came right in the house!

Question:

How do we find its owner? We would like to have it return to where it belongs. If you know of a way to kindly ask it to leave, we would appreciate it. It was a novelty at first, but now wakes everyone in the neighborhood up at the crack of dawn. OK during the week because I beat the sun up. However, I like to sleep in on weekends. Please call (###) ###-####.
Skip

8

Bits & Pieces

EATING GUINEA

Although the purpose of this book is to promote the use of guineas for gardening, there are some who are interested in tasting one, or have mentioned the possibility of selling extra keets. All comments having to do with the raising of guinea fowl are welcome on the message board on Frit's Farm. Although my theme is *Gardening With Guineas,* it is very true that these birds do multiply and all who own guinea fowl will have some to part with eventually! Whether one chooses to give away or sell excess keets, or to butcher a few older birds is a choice each individual will need to make.

Through my website, I was contacted by the owner of a new specialty restaurant and received the following letter:

To Whom It May Concern,

In the near future, I will be opening a restaurant in Boise, Indiana. I am looking for a supplier of specialty birds. Do you think you could help me? I would probably start with 2 dozen a week. I would need them very dead and cleaned. In the future, the number would probably go up. If you need any more information, let me know.

Thank you, Andrea M.

Gourmet birds are usually sold dressed and frozen to hotels and restaurants. Most are around 14-18 weeks old and weigh over 2 pounds dressed. Older guineas may be tougher and dryer.

In special cases, guineas may be marketed like game birds with the feathers still on. Guinea fowl raised for special markets are sold alive. Poultry processors then dress them like chickens.

Guinea fowl meat is drier and leaner than chicken meat and tastes similar to other game birds. It is often substituted for pheasant in finer restaurants.

Some hatcheries list the French Guinea as a "roaster" guinea. This guinea is listed as having a large body and shorter neck, and is said to be table ready in just 10 weeks.

I do not supply restaurants, am not a hatchery, nor do I raise guinea for food consumption at home. Note that there are strict laws governing hatcheries: licenses and health permits etc. required to be a hatchery or restaurant supplier that this book will not cover. The laws and restrictions in each state vary somewhat and will need to be investigated by those interested in becoming a hatchery or supplier for businesses.

Some people are unable to eat what they raise, including chickens, yet purchase those that come in a package to eat and drool over. I am one who is guilty of doing just that. When we butchered Fred, our first turkey, I could not eat turkey that Thanksgiving. I suppose you might call it "a personal problem." Nonetheless, there are many who will enjoy this section, including my own husband and son.

From, the Guinea Fowl Message Board on Frit's Farm came the following question and answers on recipes for Guinea Fowl.

RECIPE REQUEST:

Greetings from Tasmania! Would anybody out there have any good recipes on preparing guineas for the table, with emphasis on cooking duration?
Kind Regards, Michael

Re: Recipe Request

Hi, just call me "Yum-Yum" Linda, I LOVE to eat guineas. Don't get me wrong, I love my little darlings running around in the back yard and get a lot of entertainment and joy from watching them. But I have some that I put in a special pen that are designated just for eating, therefore I don't make friends with them, just feed them well. I ate them in France where they are highly esteemed for their delicate flavor. The ones I raised and eat, are so good, they don't taste like poultry, just tender delicate meat.

Here are my recipes:

ROAST GUINEA

This meat is dark and is so delicate flavored, not what you would expect, and definitely not a chicken or poultry taste. To cook it, I roasted it somewhat like a chicken:

1 Guinea serves 3 people, or 2 with great appetites.
Best when dressed at 6-8 months old.
Preheat the oven to 325 degrees F.
First I salt and pepper inside and out (Also with a little onion salt).
(Stuff if you wish - takes 15 to 20 min. longer to cook)
I sometimes stuff it with an apple.
Baste often with a mixture of 1 part White Sherry wine and 3 parts melted butter.

Cook for 25 minutes uncovered, basted and turned.
Cook an additional 25 minutes with a tin foil cover over it.
Check for doneness!
Yum, Yum

To confess, I couldn't kill or dress one of my animals. I had it done, I take the bird in a cage to a lady and go back and pick up a dressed bird, ready to eat without all of the pain. Also I never eat a friend or pet, and never the females.

BREAKFAST QUICHE

Take 2 - 3 cups of finely shredded potatoes, mix with enough vegetable oil to moisten.
Pat evenly into a pie pan as a crust, cook for 20 min. at 400 degrees or until very slightly browned.
Shred 1/2 cup of cheese, your choice, or more on bottom.
Shred or chop 1/2 to 1 cup of ham or left over guinea meat.
Beat together well 1 1/2 cups of eggs, combined with 3/4 cup of milk and 1/2 tsp. salt.
Pour over the above in pie pan.
Cook at 400 degrees about 30 min or until a knife comes out clean.
Let set for 10 minutes. Slice, and enjoy!!!

Good Luck, Linda Enger

Also in Reply for recipe requests came the following.

Re: Recipe Request

I have been experimenting with recipes for guinea hen and have found this is excellent. The whole family agrees! Which is no mean feat! Give it a try and if anyone has anymore, let me know.

We butcher the excess birds in the fall of the year; but you can do this anytime of the year, whenever your birds reach a good body/dressing weight. The method we employ is not a commercial operation but a backyard operation. The meat is not for resale to the public. In Canada, there are strict federal regulations on the slaughtering, butchering and selling of fowl. I don't think there is any difference between the two sexes in the quality of meat as long as the birds are young (1 year or less) and are healthy.

All the equipment, cleaning surfaces and holding tanks for cooling carcass are of stainless steel construction for easy and effective cleaning and sterilization. The dressing of the birds is not pleasant but standards should be followed to insure the safety of the meat, which you will be eating.

To dress a guinea fowl is exactly the same as dressing a chicken. We use a sharp axe to take the heads off and then place the carcass in cone shaped holders until the blood has drained. If the beheaded bird is left to flop around, the meat becomes badly bruised and is undesirable to eat.

The bird, when completely dead, is placed in boiling water to loosen the feathers, but we found that the guinea has very strong pinfeathers which are hard to remove. It could have been the season in which we dressed the birds and perhaps there is a better time of year to do this. As an example, geese are easier to pluck in December because of their pinfeathers (at least in our region of Canada). We have a thermo-controlled heating vat with which to heat water. That way the water doesn't get too hot or too cool. If the water is too hot the skin rips and if the water is too cool, the feathers are very hard to remove.

The carcass is then cooled, dried and placed in freezer bags. The meat is then frozen. I find the consumption of fresh meat undesirable.

Cacciatore Guinea

1. Cut up one to two guinea hens into pieces
2. Sauté guinea in 1 tbsp. of vegetable oil, until meat is no longer pink

3. Remove skin
4. Place pieces into a covered baking dish
5. Pour and stir one jar of Uncle Ben's Cacciatore Simmer Sauce[1] over meat
6. Place into 350 F oven for 45-60 minutes

**1 guinea serves 3 to 4 people

Diane Ayres, ACT
Animal Care & Veterinary Service
University of Ottawa

GUINEA TALE

The poem on the next page was posted to the Guinea Fowl Message Board just before Christmas, 1998.

---

[1] Although this was recommended, it may not be available in your area. You could prepare a Cacciatore Sauce as for a chicken. Recipes are available in some cookbooks.

'Twas the Day Before the Fair'

Twas the day before the fair, when outside the house,
All the Guineas were stirring oh what a rouse!
They mingled about, and were searching with care,
In hopes that some white millet soon would be there.
The little keets were nestled, snug in nest-beds,
While visions of millet seed ran through their heads.
And Rebel on the doorstep, and Emu further back,
Had just settled down to await their owner's snack.
When out on the lawn there arose such a clatter,
I sprang from my comp' to see what 'twas the matter.
Away out the door I flew like a flash,
Tore through the bushes, and landed with a crash.

The sun shone down upon the flowers in a row,
Giving a luster of wonder to objects below.
When what to my wondering eyes should appear,
But Emu and Rebel, with their eight tiny keets here.
With a buck and a wheat, the hens called for a treat,
I grabbed some millet, and threw it near my feet.
More rapid than eagles, those Guineas they came,
And I whistled and shouted, and called them by name.
"Come Rebel, come Emu, little keets over here,
Blackavar, Cookie, and the rest of you come near!
Go around the tree, go around to the house-wall,
Now munch away! Munch away! Munch away all!"

And when they were done, into the sky they rose,
And flying up high, my poem comes to a close.
My Guineas went roaming, and I gave a whistle,
As away they all went, across field and thistle.
But I heard someone call as they went on their way,
"Happy Gardening to all, and to all a good day!"

Christina Abramowicz

WORDS FROM AFRICA

Having met Juan and Carien Quiroga of South Africa online through the Guinea Fowl Message Board, I thought this letter from them, where Guinea Fowl are native and still roam wild, is a nice way to end the book.

• • • • • • • • • • • •

My name is Juan Quiroga, Bolivian by birth. As a youngster I had a choice to either go to the USA or Africa as an exchange student. Well I chose Africa, as it was the "continent" of my dreams.

After my year as an exchange student I decided to immigrate to this beautiful country, in Johannesburg, South Africa. Since then I have worked as a radio operator, then moved to film sound operator and worked in many wildlife documentaries, where my passion for the fauna and flora really became apparent.

I now own a small production house, making all kinds of productions. We (Carien, myself and our 3 children) live 19 miles away from Johannesburg in an agricultural holding, where we decided to get some guinea-fowls as pets. Although we heard of this "hobby" some people told us if you're lucky you will be able to "domesticate" them, but it is very unlikely. Fortunately for us, our birds seem to be quite adaptable, and as our small holding seems to be appropriate for them they made home of our place.

Guinea fowl as such are an abundant bird in South Africa. In some places they even became quite a pest, as they can be quite destructive, when they flock in their hundreds in a plantation.

Undoubtedly, the difference between a wild guinea fowl and a domesticated one is firstly their size, the wild one seems to be much slimmer and strikingly "blue" and their agility is something to challenge the most skilled hunter.

The crested guinea fowl seems to me to be the wilder of the two. Also they exist in lesser numbers or they are more shy than the helmeted ones, as I have never seen great flocks of the crested ones, perhaps a maximum of 10 to 20, always at a rush, running away from humans.

I haven't come across many guinea fowl breeders since I started breeding mine. The most fascinating one was a gentleman that incubated more than 2000 eggs per breeding season. His sole purpose was to domesticate them and release them later in the wild, for hunting purposes. That way the real wild ones would have more chances to survive than the slightly chubbier tame ones.

Although we haven't tried yet, they are revered as quite a delicacy. Guinea fowl is common on the menu in hunting lodges.

Finally, the vulturine guinea fowl is the only one that I have seen inside a cage. I have not seen any in the wild and as far as my knowledge goes they inhabit north of the equator.

Next a few domestic names for the guinea fowl, remember the difference between crested and helmeted is part of the "body language" like the index finger on top of their heads...

zulu - Mpangele
sotho - kgaka
venda - kanga
afrikaans - tarentaal

Only by becoming part of a "guinea-fowl club" on the message board did I realize that by sharing all those experiences in the African plains while on production, it became much more enjoyable to share those beautiful sights. There's nothing more beautiful than to see a flock of helmeted guinea fowl at a waterhole, almost like a school of fish, running from here to there in complete unison, apparently to catch insects that way.

It is almost impossible to describe an African sunset, with those Acacia trees in the foreground and many mysterious noises far away. The hyenas can be heard at a distance, making all different noises, from the typical laughter to some kind of howling. You can also hear lions calling, quite different from "roaring" but it is the scariest guttural sound they make, although it is quite low in frequency, it can be heard miles away.

But this picture cannot be complete without the sound of the helmeted and crested guinea fowls. It is also in early morning and at dusk times, when this concert performed by "real" and "free" wild animals occurs. If you spend a few moments with yourself, you'll discover those "dormant instincts". If you allow it you'll be hypnotized and feel drawn, almost feeling part of this performance. A twig cracking somewhere takes you away from this trance momentarily, or better still "someone" is making a kill! When these noises stop so suddenly you cannot help but feeling fear and completely helpless. The sounds and smells the wind brings are long forgotten signs and descriptions of something so foreign to us.

There's somewhere a legend that says that if you look at an African sunset for too long, you will be bewitched (blessed), and will never be able to leave Africa. Wherever you are in the world, you will always come back.

Juan Quioroga